Trickledown

Erik and Sheila in 1971

Trickledown

Poems and Contemplations

C. Erik Andren

with an introduction by
Lindy Andrén
and an appreciation by
Michael Smith

K&B

Kennedy & Boyd

Published by:

Kennedy & Boyd
An imprint of Zeticula Ltd
Unit 13
196 Rose Street
Edinburgh
EH2 4AT
Scotland

http://www.kennedyandboyd.co.uk

First published in 2019

ISBN 978-1-84921-177-2

For openers

God's Position, it is said, remains unchanging whether people believe in Him or not. The incipient author, not being blessed with omniscience, may however reasonably wonder "Will people like my book?"

It would be enviably mature to be above it all, blase, and able to declare that the answer was of no consequence, but it is! I have enjoyed writing the book, and even though it only logs today's position in my on going thoughts, I hope they might chime with yours and prove to be enjoyable.

I have also mixed the light hearted and serious fairly evenly, as life seems to do, for in laughing I have gained a great deal.

Such order as exists is simple. Generally the poems move from childhood interest to thoughtful. The prose occurs more by chance, to ambush and surprise.

And there is a current. Contentment, though much sought after is not so often found that its causes may be assumed. So I have shared thoughts and insights that have enriched and contented me.

But to begin, a fly-sheet. My impression is that fly-sheets are really not the writer's responsibility, but just in case they are, a poem about a fly on a sheet, in a book, to begin this book, should fit the occasion.

With similar eager anticipation, you and the fly both landed on "My bright white book" but I trust it will mean rather more to you than it did to him!

Erik Andren
Staines. Summer 1992

The Fly

My bright white book
Beckoned from afar,
Its gorgeous petals
Open in the sun
Like some exotic bloom
Filled with sweet promise,
Among the stamens of the print.

But when he landed
And sucked hopefully at the page
He found 'HISTORY' too dry,
No matter where he walked.

Though less exotic,
He liked my leg!*

Wellbrook, Tyrone 20 08 84

* You will appreciate that in your case I cannot offer my leg as an alternative
interest! Why not turn some pages and try dipping a little deeper instead ...

Contents

Introduction

It is more than a decade since Dad died, and the process of preparing his writing for publication has brought him roaring back to life! His vitality and twinkle leap from every page in this book as he sits alongside me, laughing and crying the memories with me.

Unusually for an author, he has been rather candid, not hiding any of his 'warts' but presenting himself with characteristic openness and honesty. In editing him I have striven to maintain his authentic voice, changing only a word of prose here or a punctuation there for clarity, much as I did in collaboration with him when he was alive. We enjoyed an unusual compatibility of mind, despite often quite fiery differences of opinion, and we revelled in that and what it brought to us both.

Also unusually, this book of poetry is a book of prose as well. Some might say that poems should stand alone, without requirement for additional text, but Dad was an interested and eager engager with life and people, seeking to share whatever communication possible at every turn. He was grounded in a simple truth: the world is all about relationship. Consequently this is a book about relationships: those between poetry and prose, and those between us and others, between us and God, and between us and the wonder of the world around us and the worlds within.

The title of the book, *Trickledown*, is also the title of the poem about wisdom on p. 188. Dad and I often spoke about titles, and this one featured regularly, seeming to encapsulate his understanding that wisdom does not come pre-packaged for easy consumption, but must be carefully condensed from life, through time and patient reflection, and allowed to flow down into the thirsty soul.

Wisdom is thus like water, gathering in the deep places and refreshing life. And water literally flows through this book. It trickles, and drips and swirls through the poems and the prose as subject, metaphor, similie and memory. For an aviator, Dad was surprisingly aquatic!

His love of words and wordplay came from his own father – another avaiator, independent thinker, and lover of laughter – who sadly died suddenly in 1972. Dad recalled his father spinning richly creative bedtime stories from such mundane things as floral wallpaper, and he continued this tradition with Ross and I, instilling in us both a love of the quirky, the upside-down and the downright silly. In this way he also gently and ably developed our critical thinking.

Humour was Dad's natural response to the world, and he loved to laugh. Dinner times were invariably chortle-laden events, often sparked by some innocent observation or casual word-play and escalating rapidly to quickfire wit and shrieks of glee. Laughter allowed him to confront the difficulties in life, to diffuse tensions and to establish quick and firm bonds with people. But he was also deeply serious, searching always for the 'gold' amongst the chaff and dross, and asking very penetrating questions. Both the deep and the delight are amply evidenced in his writing.

The book is unfinished. It is laid out in the order Dad determined, with each poem introduced by a piece of prose that either directly relates to the poem or provides an intersecting exploration of a common theme. He was steadily writing these prose pieces during the last months of his life but had not finished them when he died. The last few poems therefore stand alone, waiting for their prose partners, and we will never know what other insights and joys he would have shared. But does this make the book incomplete? I don't think so, and I don't think Dad would think so either. After all, we each remain works in progress from our first page to our last.

Lindy Andrén
Northern New South Wales, Australia, February 2019

Trickledown

Mr. Midnight

Very thin and very tall
With bent high hat to top it all
Comes Mr. Midnight calling by
While fast in dreamy sleep you lie.

In tailcoats grey with buttons three,
Each a pearl from Araby.
His shirt as white as breakfast milk,
Made soft and smooth from spider's silk.

His shanks are clad in patchwork troos
And on his feet are Elven shoes
That walk a cloud or waterfall,
Or slip him through the bedroom wall.

For every night to every bed
He comes to check each sleepy head
And bless them with a loving spell
To keep all children safe and well.

Very thin and very tall
With bent high hat to top it all
Comes Mr. Midnight calling by
While fast in dreamy sleep you lie.

Staines 24 03 92

3

From Zero to Hands-Off!

From birth we begin exploring our local area and claiming as much of it as we can hold! At first, by yelling, we only claim someone's attention, but this monocentric tendency, if unchecked, can evolve in time to the point of claiming someone's country!

The battle to socialise our offspring starts on day one and skirmishes occur, at any moment thereafter, through tots to teens and occasionally beyond into hands-off time!

Children instinctively know that parents are manoeuvrable, and that's OK within limits. But limits are limits. Unless your yea be yea and your nay be nay, and you do what you say you will do, a child learns to ignore what suits him. Step this way for anarchy and chaos!

Then there is friction. Estimating from life's encounters there are those who were not given early use of please, thank you or sorry. What they have missed! For these are life's low friction words. If you don't believe me, try life without them some time!

So the battle goes steadily on and in the end, somewhat to a parent's surprise, one begins to see signs of socially integrated adulthood in one's children. Gradually you note a willingness to accept and discharge responsibilities, and to notice and do their share of daily tasks.

Finally self discipline, with luck under an authority greater than parents or self, sets in and results in thoughtful, cooperative team people who will be good friends and well equipped parents.

But seen from the child's viewpoint learning to fit in can be VERY trying!

Two + One

Months ago When I was 'o'
Adults loved my dribbling.
From nought to two
The knowledge grew -
They'd all "Ooh Ah!" my scribbling!

I then began
My master plan
Of tantrums and of quibbling.
I beat my heels,
Upset my meals ...
Which brought about - a Sibling!

Now he is 'o'
And I just know
The adults will be dribbling
Above the cot, (Where I AM not!)
Going "Goo Ga!" at my Sibling!

So what to do
When you are two
And very strongly quibbling
With every way
Throughout the day
They idolize HIS dribbling!

A pinch should do,
(Or even two!)
To set my Sibling babbling!
Ho! Ho! the fun,
Just see them run.
And what a lot of gabbling!
"Oh! Precious dear
Your Mummy's here!"
It makes me sick, the scrabbling!
It seems to me
They just don't SEE
That I'm my brother's Sibling!

Staines 22 10 91

Crabbing

Crabs get caught because they are greedy. This is a fact and maybe a moral too, but their saving grace is that this greed makes crab line-fishing wildly exciting for young children.

On holiday in Norfolk we joined forces for a day with friends who had three very energetic young boys. Crab fishing from the narrow quay at Blakeney, set between the road and a muddy tidal creek, had all the makings of a great idea.

For a while, as the lines were set up, I sat writing in the car, parked a short distance off along the creek. From there I could see excitement growing as first one crab was lifted, then another, then two on the line, more, three, four!

With each lift the tide of excitement and the crab level in the bucket rose. The boys, including my sixteen year old, were dancing about the quay, whooping and pointing. Passers-by were readily drawn into the excitement as the crabbers, by now beyond restraint, unaware of their mothers' quaking imaginations and bone deaf to earnest entreaties, swarmed crabsomely up and down the wet woodwork of the quay to bucket the catch at water level.

I went over to see how things were a-doing, to lend general support and perhaps some gravitas. The number caught was far past the hundred and the level was thus well within crab reach of the rim, sparking even more excitement as escapees were frantically recaptured!

Eventually the whole catch was tipped back for another try and sure enough, recognised old favourites were hauled ashore again, to widespread, nigh ecstatic acclaim! The name of the game was quantity - not quality!

Whopper

I CAUGHT a crab!
I caught a crab!
I caught a crab! Just see!
I dropped a baited crab line
By the boats at Blakeney quay
And after just a minute
I caught a crab for tea!

You caught a crab?
You caught a crab.
You caught a crab for tea!
You must have caught a whopper
To feed us all for free.
So let me see the monster ...
Oh my! He's rather wee!

But Mum, he IS enormous,
With claws and stalky eyes,
The whopperingest whopper,
A really truly size,
The biggest crab I ever caught ...
Oh Mum, you must agree
He is a FAIRLY big crab,
As big as 50p!

Blakeney 14 08 90

7

Everness

The Burren in County Clare, Ireland, had long been a place I wished to visit. It is remote and beautiful, in a rugged way, with much of interest poked into crevices.

It is common knowledge that Ireland is held by some kind of spell, which the tourist trade depends on. It seems that Time itself has been arrested for loitering, for failing to do its job properly, and charged with intent to waylay passers-by.

The arrest of time gives Ireland an everness. It might also be why the 'Little People' can still be felt there; they have simply not been vacuumed up by chronometry, atomic clocks or the odd idea that time runs out!

Children also live in an everness where time has little sway, but everness is not quite real, and nor does childhood last. Even in Ireland, Time will be given bail and let out again.

Then, instead of 'experiencing' and 'being' one has to start 'knowing' and 'planning'. Everness ends. One has to integrate with time, to decide things, to know and name things, to be clear and to define oneself.

Away slips the gossamer of simple days and innocence.

'Whatnot'

I think I'll be a 'whatnot', 'cos I
just don't seem to be
One of what the OTHERS are; they're none of them quite 'ME',
It's all a bit confusing, I think you understand,
Growing up uncertain of exactly where you stand!

I'm not a sly eyed Chinaman from by the Yellow Sea.
That would be exciting ... , but I don't like China tea!
I'm not a turbaned Arab, with some camels and a tent,
And glinting teeth for grinnnnning and a great brown nose,
   that's bent.
I'm not a skinny fakir with a bedspring made of nails.
I'm not a dancing master with a cane and faded tails.
But I could be a Policeman with a radio and truncheon,
And ride around in Panda cars, with sandwiches to munch on.

Perhaps, a Roman soldier, with a helmet down my nose,
Roaming over everywhere a Roman soldier goes?
But then, I doubt I could be, as I'm not quite OLD enough
For serving as Centurion and being rather gruff.

Might I be Brazillian? Or a man from far Fiji?
Or an Indian with vermilion on my forehead? Possibly!
But what about my parents? They're frightfully important,
And often help me stop myself becoming what I oughtn't!

Do I come from hidden jungles, from a dismal heathen home?
Can I melt into the landscape, like a Fairy or a Gnome?
I can do that very neatly when its time for bath or bed,
But I don't much fancy jungles; so I'm someone else instead!

I'm not a skirted Grecian, or from Java or Johore,
I'm not a Dane or Fresian, nor a man from hot Mysore!
But 'WHAT' is what is needed, I'm sure as sure can be,
And I must find out quickly, so that I can grow up me!

But while I keep on looking, .. a 'whatnot' might be best.
It makes the choosing easier, by leaving out the rest!
So while I keep on looking, I'm a 'whatnot', just from 'HERE'
While all the other people are a 'someone' just from 'THERE'!

That's sorted out the puzzle!
That's clear at last!
You see, I
must be, just be,
Who I AM!

I must be, just be - ME!

Burren/Staines 22-26 July 89

Freedom

An eleven year old contemporary of my son was the 'cause' of this poem. On a very hot outing to a Shire Horse Centre in Devon he had quietly and resolutely refused anything to drink. It was clear the lad knew his mind and for whatever reason was not to be moved. It underlined a point for me about a popular concept - freedom.

I wonder what is understood by the word. Is the lack of limits freedom? What makes a person free?

Limitlessness is not freedom, that soon imposes on those who seek it a tyranny of meaningless chaos. Instead I see freedom stem from the individual's ability to disagree, and say "no", against a clear set of self imposed standards which, paradoxically, set limits on his behaviour.

There are two factors here. First, agreement or otherwise requires that alternative choices exist, and also the means for evaluating them, in other words: information and understanding. Second, the matter of capability. Can one hold to one's standards and say "no"?

Where choices or information are withheld, freedom is impeded, perhaps even withdrawn, but freedom is abandoned when one's ability to say "no" fails. Then one is swept on by the acquiescent tide, willy nilly!

When the lad said "no thank you", he had evaluated information and made his choice. When he held to it he went beyond the reach of my adult power to influence his resolve. On that point he became free of me, his own man.

Centre Stage

I once knew a boy, of ten summers, I think,
Who decided one day to never more drink.
His mother grew anxious. She said he was "Bad!"
"I give you fair warning; I'm telling your Dad!"
"What's the Lad doing?" Ranted his father.
"If he simply won't drink he'll not get much further!"
At bed time that evening the boy went to bed;
His parents predicted he'd forget what he'd said.
But at breakfast next morning, and with twinkling eye,
The lad had his cornflakes, EXCEEDINGLY dry!

The boy was like granite and NOT going to budge.
So they called in the Doctor and asked him to judge.
The Doctor looked solemn, and prodded and poked.
Then said to the patient that he NEVER joked.
"The matter is weighty; but to keep 'in the pink'
It is simply IMPERATIVE for people to drink!"
He refused fizzy orange! He refused Cola too!
He just ate dry biscuits, and wouldn't take stew!
He would NOT take water. (He wouldn't take beer!)
And refused all advice. He just WOULDN'T hear!

The days ran to weeks. The weeks ran to years!
The boy was not thirsty, or so it appears!
He was 'old' at thirteen, (As dry as a prune!)
All brown and wrinkled, quite parched, like a dune!
But he wouldn't take Perrier and he spurned Soda Pop!
He jibed at all juices. He touched NOT A DROP!
The plied him with porter, cold cocoa, brown ale!
But all of their efforts were destined to fail.

He didn't drink! He wouldn't drink! The Doctors washed their
    hands
And issued a disclaimer about chaps and swollen glands.
The medical profession decided in this case
That the lad would not have long among the Human Race!
THEN, as if to show them, as quickly as wink,
The boy just decided he'd have a QUENCHING drink!

He guzzled some glasses of very strong juices.
He opened some cans and found some new uses
For a bucket and barrel, and then the fish pond!
He drank all in sight and most things beyond!
They had to restrain him when he reached the sea,
And on some reflection he did then agree
With the pleas of his parents, (And his very best friend)
To start acting NORMAL, and bring to an end,
(For the while at least) his behaviour daft.
He's now circumscribing the World ... on a raft!

Plymouth 30 10 85

Evaporated Time

These lines are separated from those on the next page by nine years. Plenty happens to children in that time! At eleven and nine they flew to 'Grandma New Zealand' without us. Six weeks later they returned walking tall and self assured.

Now, such apron strings as were required are all but loosed. Teenage development and growth was achieved via negotiation rather than rebellion. Listening, talking and laughing together proved a sound framework, but it has not been all downhill!

Ross now towers above me and is lithe and open. Lindy is a zesty young woman, with keen sensitivity and insight. Both are quick and witty good company, but only a breath or two ago they were ten and eight!

How do you hold onto such a precious time? It slips through the gaps in my memory so easily that even familiar photographs somehow seem to be of other children.

Photographs freeze a moment. For me this little poem breaths life back into that fleeting time and those frozen impressions.

Ten & Eight

The girl is growing,
Shooting into maidhood,
Filling like a summer
Bursting with wild flowers,
Often tatty in detail
But beautiful over all.

Small wonder I'm in love.
How could a father resist
The shy try-out sauce,
The flirt unconscious —
Automatic in the process
Of waking into womanhood.

And the boy. Quite another love.
Pride and future man mingle
In this feeling for his warmth
And small frame ruggedness.
Willing, friendly, light voiced,
He robusts into my life -
At every opportunity.

Staines 30 07 82

In Walton

It was a still late spring evening in the south of England. The sun golden, low and lukewarm, the air sweet with new bloom.

It was too good to miss after winter so Ross and I went out for a drive. But small boys need exercising so I stopped as we went through Walton-on-Thames, by the Council Offices which stand on the edge of a parkland in the town.

As I parked Ross saw the tree and its fallen blossom and broke from the car as we stopped. I sat a while watching him cavort in the slanting light.

It was only slowly that I recalled schooling in Walton during the Second World War. I was only four or five, but there were positively ancient boys in the school too, of eleven!... and a bird-bath fountain, and... and...

Then, as waves of recollections poured out of memory's trenches, one made straight for me and passed through this occasion like a shade, giving it unexpected significance.

Father and Son

Here, upon this Municipal sward,
Razor trim at every edge,
One flagrant tree
Standing in a pretty pool
Of lost pink petticoats
Lets fall her blossom
With artless airy grace
And yet holds some about her.

This maiden brazen tree
Is not lost upon the boy.
He loves her; ecstatically,
Innocent as eight can be.
Scooping high her pink flounces
They bomb-burst
From his high flung hand
And spangle down through sun shafts,
Flecking his eager face
With taffeta kisses:
Promises, falling at his feet
As he whirls this courtship dance:
To the tree. To the sun.
To life itself.

And as I watched, again I smelt
The damp ditch bottom of long past.
Verdant, pungent, weed crushed smells,
And the gall of being frightened,
By a proxy fear, not my own.

One shout had been enough
To fling the crocodile of children
Into cover, cowering from
The on-coming flying bomb.

Here, upon this same Municipal sward
It burst, in full burst blossom time,
And shook Creation by the throat
In its moment of power.

And the high flung blossom fell, torn,
Yet with pregnant promise
For this, God's future,
With my son.

Staines 16 05 83

In Windsor Great Park

Our children's school was having its annual day out in Windsor Great Park. Everyone had been given a choice of activity and teams of suitably equipped children were scouring about dipping in ponds, stalking fungi, counting thingummies or otherwise engaged in omnidirectional running around designed to keep teachers busy, fulfilled and exhausted.

My wife had been asked to be 'Doctor on hand' should there be any cases of overlong submersion, over-enthusiastic tasting, over-ambitious gravitational assessments, or any other over-diligent educational activity that might result in more than mildly impaired performance! I took the afternoon off to sit and chat, keeping her company in the sun.

Through the buzzy sun meadow murmurings and then into earshot ran a distant snatch of children chaffing about what cannibals did and did not eat. Apparently no vegetables. The know-all from second year was helping some hapless child feel the full weight of his or her ignorance on the point: "Didn't you know that! Silly!"

The hotly-held mis-information amused me and set me writing.

Neighbourhood Cannibal

I'm a cannibal!
Yes, a cannibal!
I live just up your street,
But I keep it very quiet
From the people that I meet.
(I know it tends to frighten
So I have to be discreet!)
They seem to think a cannibal
Sees THEM as good to eat!

But people are so prejudiced,
Their thinking goes to POT!
I'm not that sort of cannibal,
They ought to know I'm not!
I chew my fingers, bite my nails
I sometimes pick my nose!
I'm not a frightening cannibal;
Not as a cannibal goes!

In fact - I'm vegetarian
By conviction and belief!
Which, according to my neighbours,
Affords them great relief!

Smith's Lawn 06 06 84

Root Bound?

On our kitchen window sill stood a small pot of asparagus fern. It had been part of a potted-up selection which, for lack of adequate attention, light or water on the hall table, had resolved to die.

Before it succeeded it had been re-potted, in hope, with a view to what looked like resurrection. The fern, represented now only by some thin, green, leaf-lacking stalks, was being willed into making a comeback in the light, and close to the sink.

Pondering this fern over the rim of my coffee cup I mused that plants, particularly those given to us, relied on a rather risky, rooted, strategy for survival, expecting to 'find' their needs just where they happened to be, unless like duckweed they were adrift. Animals with their mobile, 'hunting' strategy, even it is only for fresh fodder, control their fate far better.

Perhaps some of the really unstoppable, successful plants are mobile too… Hmm?

Deadly Night Shade

The shade of night is upon us!
'Tis time to tell stories in bed.
So, careful as careful, just listen,
As this caution'ry tale is read!

Beware of the Dangerous Daisy!
And the Deadly Dandelion too!
As you stroll in the shade of evening,
Look out for the Bad Bamboo!

They thrill as they sense your footfall
And tremble with sappy glee,
These perilous packs of hunting plants
Are planning to have you for tea!

They will stalk, and freeze, and scuttle,
They will ravel you up in their roots;
Digest you down to the wishbone
And leave just your bones and boots!

They linger in day-long ambush,
For the glim of the evening shade,
Then they loom on the lawn to grab you!
A fate that is hard to evade!

So beware the Dangerous Dandelion,
With its yellow fanged head!
The sight will afright and fill you
With panic, and nightmares of dread!

The Bad Bamboo will entrap you!
By luring you into its stand,
Then closing its stalks all around you ...
Except for your out-stret-t-tching hand!

And when you walk on windy hills
The Deadly Daisy knows!
Their red stained teeth just gently grin,
At the sight of your sandaled toes!

And the word goes out that you are about
And the Daisies knowingly smile.
"Here comes - here comes one sucking his thumbs!
A tasty treat - in a while!"

They wait in the day, so prettily,
Dreaming of evening, and all ...
The hunting, stalking, and catching!
When they sense your passing footfall!

So take heed, as the sun starts dipping!
Take heed! Don't scream or create!
Stop sucking your thumb and listen to Mum ...
"There is ONLY one way ...
.   ..AAGGHHHhhhhh ... !!
                              ... too late!"

Staines 21 03 91

Chef d'Oeuf

By great good fortune, Sheila cooks for fun, for when I married her I knew not if she could boil an egg. Fortunately she can, for I have been known to fumble that endeavour! On one occasion five par-cooked eggs were found in various states of dribbling decapitation on the kitchen worktop following such an attempt.

I had carefully followed what I understood to be the rules for egg boiling but despite attentive timing I consistently failed to achieve albumenic solidity! The experience left me uneasy. Should I feign an indignant wrath about 'the effect of summer time on the boiling point of northern hemisphere tap water' etc. and thus risk muffing it again in future, or should I shelter under the ample rock of my culinary ineptitude? Sheila's scientific and kitchen qualifications opted me for ineptitude, where I regret to say I have remained.

So I am impressed by cooking and to compensate in some small way for my shortcomings I truly appreciate (almost) everything that is put before me, and even eat left-overs gratefully next day.

Marble pie, the recreational kind not the monumental sort, is a Sheila special that I love. Others call it gooseberry pie, but just look at the apathetic way pastry reclines over the contents. My children KNEW it was marble pie the first time they set eyes on it!

As will be seen overleaf, not only can I not cook, I don't spell too good either!

Toothsome

Tweecle, tweecle little sponge,
How I like you for my lunge.
Then again I'd rate quite high
A mighty slab of marble pie!

Staines 18 05 84

Out of Stock

Life sometimes, and always unexpectedly, ambushes one with a question for which an answer is rather immediately needed but for which an answer is clearly out of stock! The questioner awaits enquiringly while we feverishly endeavour to cobble up a workable jury rig.

The truth is we feel silly and inadequate at times like these and inadequacy is not one of the things we hoist bunting about.

But there is nothing unusual or even shameful about inadequacy. It is perhaps our native and predominant state! What do we really know, even about our own subject? I guess one needs to accept the feeling and ask more questions, but then there is the problem of cranky memory…!

Tongue Tied

The word is on the tip of my tongue ...
I'll get it in a little ... ,
I know it's there,
Just give me time ...
Ah yes! Of course!
It's -
'Spittle'!

Staines 22 12 91

Fourteen Thoughts

Musing as I watched rain spike past my window, it seemed to me that the sky really did leak quite badly! It was a fourteen sort of thought so I smiled, on the private side of my face, and wrote about it for my daughter's fourteenth birthday.

I recall being fourteen. Grown, well almost; full, with the grasp of things unknown to my parents at fourteen, and yet a bit uncertain about the fall of childhood and the spring of adolescence.

Anyone can be fourteen, if they see the world with untrammelled wonderment, but for many people fourteen remains only as a distant fact, indeed it's clear that some people never ever were fourteen, but I didn't write this for them, so that's alright!

Air Apparent

Air is thin, and full of holes.
It lets in rain, and fills up bowls.
It connects us up with outer space,
And to all the Human Race.
It trembles with sound, vibrates with song,
It's sometimes perfumed, or filled with pong!
It's hard as rock at the speed of sound,
But soft as a kiss when whispered around.
It's everywhere where something isn't.
It fills up the cracks another thing doesn't!
It's there, but air isn't always apparent.
Some things are, while others aren't!
But by and large, (there's quite a mass!)
The air we share is quite a gas!

Staines 20 02 86,
for Lindy

Intro to the Artiste

"Oh look!" said my daughter, "a performing biscuit!"

Lindy is the tea drinker in our coffee-centred family, she is also the great biscuit dunker. Each afternoon when the family get in, we tend to gather for a drink and catch-up in the kitchen.

And so it was: Lindy, mug before her and a highly absorbent 'Shrewsbury' biscuit on the table balanced on edge, just awaiting its big moment.

The repertoire of biscuits being generally what it is, this one was crimped edges and currants ahead of the field...

Lindy

"Duncan" - The Performing Biscuit

My Lords, Ladies and Gentlemen,
(Lads and Lassies too!)
It is with the greatest of pleasure,
We present our next Act for you.
We know that before you have seen him
You'll wonder whether he'll risk it
For tonight, Dear Folks, we present ...
"Duncan" - the Performing Biscuit!
He will fill you ... With anticipation!
He will leave you ... With jaws ajar!
This Artiste, on the rim of a teacup,
Admired by all from afar!
He will plunge with panache amazing,
(As all of us gathered will see)
And emerge a few moments later ...
Unharmed from the broiling tea!
Then soggy and slumped from his ducking,
He will wave! (to acknowledge your cheers!)
Then head for your gape in a flabbier shape,
To join the cream filled eclairs!
We know that before you have seen him
You'll marvel that he will risk it,
But then, not all have the courage ...
Of "Duncan" - the Performing Biscuit!

Staines 21 03 91
Dedicated to Lindy, who sparked the fun and laughed with me.

Child-Like

If you are crafty, Growing Up can be avoided. Naturally, ten will always come after nine, and fifty follows forty with hectic speed, but that is only age.

I'm talking about attitude. It is to childlike, not childish qualities that I wish to cling. Children see with a perception, freshness and wonderment that is easily lost. And what a real loss it is.

I don't mind getting older or being a bit stiffer of limb. I'm ready enough to mature, crumble a bit, or even wear the wisps of wisdom should they settle, but I simply refuse to grow up!

I want to know the lifelong wonderment and thrill of childhood. Who wants sophisticated adulthood if it patiently pats childhood's head, and misses the fun and transparency of new wonder? How dull!

Children love the anarchy of nonsense because it sharpens their appreciation of sense! At the "What noise does a... make?" stage, my children went into kinks when suddenly the butterfly went "Brooum, Brooum!" and the elephant went "Eeeek!"

So without apology but in gratitude to Jabberwocky and everything else that makes delicious, magic nonsense...

Gribwang

Beyond the Great Aclastic,
Harbide the single Cree,
Stood the Moaning Bunntak
With foaming slaverjee

By came the Nagle Gribwang
Croilling his armour bright
Then thurbed the Moaning Bunntak
A thurb of mighty might!

The Bunntak grove with shudders
The weildy crash to stand
And parged the Nagle Gribwang
With classic blatherband.

A full elack the trummill last,
And then another quord,
Until the Slading Orb was still,
And none could say a word.

Then weapled and in purveyal,
All dinging and bereft,
Lefangiously the Bunntak lay -
Thus was the Gribwang left.

And so it was the Gribwang
Attained the single Cree
Far verder than the Everlast
O'er thunderous Blasterbre.

Staines 28 04 91

To Me It's a Haemorrhage!

I'm into cowardice not sang-froid when it comes to blood tests. I much prefer my sang-chaud in regular sanguiferous channels!

"Roll up your sleeve" activates elaborate automatic circuits of isolating valves in my veins. Blood is rapidly diverted from the arm in question, the vessels collapse out of sight leaving the flesh marbly.

"Let's see the other arm."

Immediately the haematic excess lurking in that engorged pink limb departs for inner sanctuaries such as the small intestine. Meanwhile, I quake.

The whole thing now becomes very serious. The phlebotomist nods the knowing nod of long experience. These sepulchral limbs are clearly a direct, perhaps even a flagrant challenge to their very raison d'être. Grudge I do not need!

The ensuing are not merry minutes. To trap some fleeing blood a limb is tourniquetted, but too late. Only dregs remain. To maintain an air of confidence, various draw-off sites are then closely surveyed and a bold decision made. In goes the probe, Ow!, to guddle about for blood. But alas! In it goes again, Ow!, alas, and again, OW!

Five a side phlebotomy is the maximum. You then run out of digits with which to staunch the resulting wounds. If they use both arms to catch some fugitive flow, you end up twisted, but should easily span an octave!

Eventually enough blood is trapped and hostilities cease. Limbs immediately glow ruddy again as normal flow is resumed.

Time now for a Heroic Stance. "Look at that!" I said indignantly pointing at the floor on one occasion. "Oh that doesn't matter, we'll soon wipe that up."

Some people have no feelings!

Phlebotomised

She came, she saw, she punctured.
I winced, I reeled, I bled.
She sucked, she wiped, she squirted.
I breathed, I pressed, I fled!

Staines 06 12 91

Eleven, and Still Scared — Baltimore

I recall as a spindly eleven year old we sailed from Singapore by cargo boat via Cibu and Legaspi in the Phillipines, picking up copra, then across the non-Pacific Ocean to Los Angeles.

Railroads, the 'Noon Daylight' and 'Overlander', took us to San Francisco and from Oakland, on the east bay shore, to Chicago – days away.

I reached Johns Hopkins Hospital, Baltimore, in early 1950. The hospital was pioneering heart surgery and I needed help. They did the tests, read the results, and were reluctant. But a man at Guy's Hospital, London, might be able to help. We moved on to see him, and he helped.

Baltimore left me without a silver dollar, missing from my bedside locker, and with my most painful memory. Arterial blood was ineptly taken from my right groin. It hurt!

Forty one years on cardiac angiography via the right groin was required. Techniques had changed but not my memory! An inner eleven year old began yelling and the rational fifty three year old could not stop him!

The day came and I felt very craven and foolish, but it is amazing how powerful care is and how it can show itself in such sudden abundance. First the gentle ones who looked after me, then the fact that technology really had moved on. I barely felt a thing!

Gentle One

Oh! Gentle one, there is in you
The dwelling of the Lord,
And busy though you are each day,
Through you His voice is heard.

Oh! Gentle one, the little boy
Inside me was afraid,
And busy though you were that day
Through you, my peace I made.

Oh! Gentle one, my fears you saw
And held them as your own,
And busy though you were that day
Through you was courage grown.

Oh! Gentle one, I thank you
For your compassioned hand,
For busy though you were that day
It's clear - you understand.

Oh! Gentle one, my future fills
With prospects hard to face,
But busy though you are each day
Through you - will come His Grace.

Staines 04 05 91
Dedicated to Megan on D. East.
Gaye in Theatre.

Sketchy Conversations

Some years ago I designed a prestigious sales shop in Rome for an Arab airline. It was one of a series commissioned along their routes, but this one was a real challenge.

In all the other cities of North Africa and Europe where I built facilities even the foremen spoke useable English, but in Rome I was expected to do as the Romans do, but I couldn't!

With no common language available, the months ahead looked fraught indeed. But the project went very well, even without mishap. Other human qualities came into play which built a rich communication that only lightly relied on the spoken word.

With common purpose, technical insight, patience, good will, sketching, body language, signs, humour, gratitude for the other's efforts, and understanding for their difficulties, we developed teamwork, respect, frankness, trust and – a fine shop!

Everyone on site joined in and amid the struggle to convey our purposes each one became the source of much laughter as ideas were reduced to simple, often quite basic form! But we did it.

Language is useful for subtleties, but not necessary for basic understanding. We used man's universal interest in understanding the other fellow and the hopes, gestures, experiences, and expressions known to all humanity.

The sounds and syntax of a language are but cultural choices evolved thought time and usage to codify man's common experiences for easy use. An unknown language is not nonsense, and if we are immersed in it our common experiences soon begin to decipher the bones of its meaning. Similarly, senseless sounds in the style of one's own language may provide unexpected imagery.

The Jilicious Maid

"Alack! Alack!" His wavled claim,
"Alack! She mulloes me,
For her adule I cannot win!
O! frantish patricey!"

So the mimpling swain rove up
And in the clistering een
Let plather all his penshus hope
That it, by her, be seen.

"a! Jilicous maid, I adudore,
And prosterly place you fair,
So haste, diratch your chasserent,
Dnfrane your rillifous hair!"

From limsome phansery woke the maid
On hearing this tender trone,
And wenderly threw the swain a rose
Close by her panifauld grown.

"a! Maid, a! maid, don't naithy so
For it doth grammle me cruel!
My fimbulous heart is all I have
For to win your fair adule!"

The winkering moon from cloud to cloud
Did dark and glim altate,
And by its boemous shade it let
The swain and the maid relate!

"a! Jilicous maid, I adudore,
And prosterly place you fair.
Come be my love this aftermore,
For we are a trusslecum pair!"

Staines 19 08 91

Detailed Observation!

This poem was written on holiday, sitting alone in the sun, shaded by an overhung branch, on a folding chair set on a large flat rock in the middle of the river Ballinderry, in Northern Ireland.

A line of mature trees sat sighing on one bank with their feet cooling in the stream and their knees showing. Beyond them lay a wide pasture cropped to the contour by dedicated cows. The other bank was bald save for some bramble stubble here and there. A slight silt-made levee sloped back into a boggy flaxen meadow.

I sat for about two hours very quietly observing these surroundings, the fish, the intimate detail of the river and its business, and was lucky enough to see a stoat quarter the bank for food.

Entomologists among you, particularly those for whom the order Diptera is an open book, may well be able to identify the hero of my poem. He set down on my pad and I have described him and his behaviour with care.

It was a prolific afternoon, full to ecstasy with summer. On that rock I wrote a number of poems. Then, to my great and gawping surprise, a squad of about ten fully armed British soldiers prickly with equipment simply de-camouflaged out of my surroundings, waved to me cheerily and trudged off to ambush some other suspicious sunny meadow!

I had no idea that the espionage theme was quite so appropriate!

Double oo Fly

Here comes a very small fellow,
Black as a coal hole at night,
Slight as an ant - but not yellow;
His courage would give you a fright!

His wings he could fold - if he chose to,
But prefers to keep 'working' instead,
So while he walks he waves them,
Like Indian Clubs, round his head.

And look at that walk! He means business!
He's off to a rendezvous
With someone from 'M' or from 'UNCLE'
(But I'm just too big to be true!)

So he walks with the motor running
Just in case there's a nasty surprise;
But you'd need to think twice to cross him
Having seen the glint in his eyes!

Then with a leap he is airborne;
Off to the next urgent call,
A micro-dot fixed to each wing tip
Over which Nations will fall!

He is brave. He is cunning and stealthy,
His methods are subtle and sly:
If espionage is your business -
The Agent to fear is Bond-Fly!

Wellbrook, Tyrone 20 08 84

It's the Done Thing

The 'Done Thing' provides auto-navigation for certain people. Switch it on and one may move from 'a' to 'b' and beyond with little need for personal input – adequate social navigation is assured. One may rest easy that gaffes (pardon me - *faux pas!*) are unlikely, and be confident of one's position and social correctness. In short, the 'done thing' gives the semblance of manners, even be they absent.

Because it is a patent medicine the done thing remains unquestionable, no matter how dotty, until the formula is changed! Do the done thing automatically, and one becomes predictable, a regular chap, and thus easily acceptable. The done thing must have the orthodoxy of a Gentlemen's London Club, and a touch of Sparta, and that's the end of it!

Only certain established 'eccentrics' (ie. those who actually do possess elegant manners or very great wealth) can navigate as they will and be acceptable. Subtle Great Circle courses of the well mannered are aped by lesser social navigators who reduce them to easily followed rhumb lines, for rapid inclusion in the orthodoxy. It's all part of the British stiff upper lip.

Stiff Upper

We're British you know,
So we will enjoy
This fete worse than death;
This rain soaked ploy
To lighten our pockets of our Pounds,
On thinly religious, Church Fete grounds.

The stall in the corner
Is going great guns
With herbal cures
And sticky buns
While the stand with the jam
Has huge reserves -
"Oh Lord preserve us
From Preserves!"

The Mayor is here
With his ball and chain;
And the local Tarzan
With the latest Jane,
And we'll all be here
Next year again
Doing 'our bit'
In the pouring rain!

So soaked to the skin
We'll gambol and hoot,
We'll toss a sponge or hurl a boot,
And in the tea tent, steaming stand
Saying "Isn't this year's Church Fete grand!"
While discerning with our inner eye,
Our feteful, social, outright lie!
"But!" says your conscience,
"you're British, m' lad,
And the British enjoy fetes,
No matter how bad!"

So.
I will, You will,
We will enjoy!
And not let the weather, our fun alloy!
We WILL enjoy it!
We WILL enjoy!!
In the name of our forefathers.

Amen!

Staines 19 09 85

Dressing

It is a fortuitous point that I was born steady British not chic French, for perhaps you have noticed the regular absence of my name from the list of The World's 100 Best Dressed Men. To find me you have to search near the end of the list of The World's More Unremarkably Dressed Men. Why? Quite simple. I have scant time for fashion and am satisfied if clothes are comfortable, clean, practical, harmonious, and in fair repair.

I tend to settle for shoes that I like and then wear them daily until they need replacement. If they were comfortable and wore well I will happily buy another pair.

The same tendency pertains to trousers, shirts, suits etc., but my wife, seeing the potential for dementia in ironing three rotating copies of the same shirt for months on end, wrested the initiative for clothes buying from me early in the marriage, and has remained sane.

I must confess though, there are elegant occasions when being well groomed and turned out does matter to me, and then I dress with care. But even so it is not fashion that attracts me so much as good design. I guess that fashion does not appeal to the designer in me, it does not set out to satisfy a need so much as focus attention and pamper passing whims.

"But," I hear my children say, "from where we stand your clothes sense is quite as whimsical. Even square"

"Ah! Well now. That's established whimsy and besides, lacerated jeans are drafty. Did you say you had finished your homework?"

Ubiquitous

The common, useful plastic bag
Will safe convey one's shopping swag,
Or cover hair when ere the sun
Should disappear and rain should run
Cascading down upon one's hair
Had one had to leave it bare!

You are never undressed,
With a plastic bag!
"You haven't a beach dress?"
"Haven't a rag!"
I've seen them used
You'll never guess,
Modified to form a dress:
Arms under handles,
Head through the two,
Snip with the scissors
and poke legs through!
For bashful belles
Upon the beach,
There's Haute Couture,
At five pence each!

There are bags for the freezer,
Bags for the bin.
Bags for carrying goldfish in!
Bags with zips or self sealing seams
There's bound to be a bag of your dreams!
Bags with holes in, others with string;
Bags over pot plants
Speeding up spring!

Life on the whole must have been a drag
Before this all enveloping bag,
But thank your stars, they now have made
Plastic bags that biodegrade!

Wellbrook, Tyrone 10 08 84

I'll Tak the Low Road

Scotland. Ah! Kilts and oatcakes, monsters, porridge, glens and strathspeys, cabers and Lochs. As is only to be expected, Scotland is full of its unique way of doing things.

I married a Glasgow lass and so have had quite a long, regular and most enjoyable connection with Scotland and the Scots. I have lived on "yon bonnie banks" overlooking Loch Lomond and have spent many happy hours poised over spectacular countryside alone in a glider, amazed that such variety and ruggedness can be achieved in so small a compass.

Open a map and be enchanted by the names. Open a door and be welcomed by a warmth that is not so natural in some other places I know. Open a malt and share a dram or two to enter into the heart and philosophy of your companion.

But for all this I feel the Scots can be a little intense. It shows in their traditional songs as a sense of wistful lament, as if the 'dour Scot' was the only kind of bard about. Even jigs and airs feel tinged with it and a mood of vague guilt seems easily assumed.

But then what do I know, I just gently pull their leg, and they smile broadly.

The Bogle Lament

Bogle! o Bogle! Come back to the glens;
Forgive us for what we did wrong.
Return to the neuks where first you took breath;
And sing your mellifluous song!

Weep? Aye, we weep for the days of old yore,
And wonder, "How will we go on,
If children can't hear a Bogle sing song,
To a kirk-bell, chanter and gong?"

Search? Aye, we search by the Sound of Drumspin
And all down the Braes o' Cairn Gruke
But nowhere it seems the Bogle still sings,
'Tween the Kirtles of Inch and Strathpluke.

Look? Aye, we look by the Bridges of Boyce
And well past the Well of McPhrail,
As far as the Falls of Trummle Loch Ar,
And the Kyles of Kintle and Sale.

Rove? How we rove through the Forests of Gart,
O'er trails on the Haughs of Benspune
But search as we might the BogIes took fright,
For we've not heard their marvellous tune.

Lament? Aye, lament! The glens give no joy,
And the Firth of Clachan Lochknee
Seems grey as the day they first went away
O BogIes! O Where can you be!

Bogle! o Bogle! Come back to the glens;
Forgive us for what we did wrong.
Return to the neuks where first you took breath;
And sing your mellifluous song!

Staines 27 05 92

Eccentricity

Eccentricity is a British quality worthy of preservation. It provides seasoning for daily life, raises some living landmarks, makes for amusement, and even facilitates progress!

Not so long ago British eccentricity was seen as a virtue – odd, quirky, sometimes downright irritating, but none the less a virtue. The eccentric was seen to have freed himself from the shackles of convention and to have moved into a world awash with individuality and opportunity, much to the envy of the more conservative.

Today eccentricity is not so much appreciated. It cannot be quantified, defies categorisation, and is in short, aberrant. It messes up the tidy, digitised, predictable acountancy of tunnel visioned uniformity and is thus administratively irritating and disruptive!

But long live quirky eccentricity! We all need some if life is to be lived to the delicious giddy full, somewhat off-centre!

Eccentricity, the valuable enjoyable kind, is personal and carefree not care-less of others. It is not about imposing or depriving or aggression. It is not anarchy on a grand scale, but simply one's declaration of independence, of unique rebellion against conforming for the sake of bureaucratic convenience or even convention.

One of my minor eccentricities is long cotton socks. I like them, summer or winter, temperate or tropics and I am prepared to go a long way to get them, if I can…

Longing Socks

Summers four and forty past
Have brushed my knees as any stream
But now I find myself aghast
By some problem from a dream!

Now you may smile - and some have mocked,
But you see - I am unsocked!

This plight has crept upon me slow
For I, unwitting, did propose
To buy some more, when these socks go
The way of all well worn old hose.

Now, antique chairs with legs baroqued
Stand unadorned - but I'm unsocked!

Now I'm a man of modest measure,
Not too tall and not too squat,
So shorts in summer are my pleasure,
When the weather gets too hot.

Now at my shins eyebrows are cocked,
For they see - I am unsocked!

With trousers long one wears socks short,
But when in shorts I feel it wrong
To wear socks - as though for sport,
Or any other how - but long!

So now my poise is badly rocked,
For you see - I am unsocked.

In days gone by I'd clad my calf
In cotton socks with fancy top.
I'd never do such things by half
But now all that has got to stop,

For all my efforts have been blocked.
It seems the world wants me unsocked!

For nowhere in this Ancient Land
Can socks to clad my thews be bought!
I've tried to make them understand
It's long socks I want - not short!

But nowhere now is such hose stocked,
So I am doomed to stay unsocked!

So while I scour each Haberdasher
For a last lost lurking pair,
My walking out - once bold - is rasher
Now my toes and heel appear!

(I feel the shame as if unfrocked!)
And all because I am unsocked!

And should I find one lurking pair,
Would I brave the vendor's eye,
Or don long pants and with an air
Buy - and rush them home to try!

Were they cotton - ribbed or smocked,
I'd have them, for I am unsocked!

So here I am quite near demented,
Pondering this paradox:
They can't be bought - or even rented!
So HOW to get long cotton socks!

Now you may smile - and some have mocked,
But you see - I am unsocked!

Scotlandwell 06 08 82

Footnote.
No more shall I, this Ancient Land,
Parade with tater'd toes outpoked,
or from an Antipodian hand
Has come my rescue - as if bespoked!
The 'walking socks' fit sheer and white,
(The Dover cliffs aren't half so bright!)
And never more will I be mocked
For now again - I AM re-socked!

Staines 30 08 82

" ... Like a Native!"

"Lingua franca. A mixture of It., Fr., Gk., Sp., and Arab. Once a common tongue in the Levant."

Despite not being very franca, English, rich in words pinched, plundered, or purloined from other languages and used world wide as a common tongue, now qualifies as the new lingua franca.

Now that is easy for anglophones, but tough on those learning to be, or just trying to understand the natives. And made tougher because the meaning often depends on how things are said rather than what is said! Double English seems rather fairer than double Dutch!

If you were not born British or you struggle with how we use our language, perhaps you should turn the page, resist temptation, overlook this poem and move on. If you don't you run the real risk of being...

Left Right Behind!

As I left for home last night
The man I left was not quite right.
I saw he had - but one leg left
But also had - but one leg Right!
He had had his Left leg left
Thus his Left leg would be right,
And he had his Right leg left
So his Right leg too, was right!
'Twas clear - he had his Left leg left!
And his Right leg was all right!
So both his legs were clearly left,
While both his legs were clearly right!
As I left for home last night
The man I left was quite alright
You see he had - but one leg Left
But also had - but one leg Right!

Staines 28 04 91

Tramp Leaning

On the whole I prefer thought to sport, mainly because I was not a healthy child. Thankfully, not so my children. So while they rush about being active, I get lost for hours in the study, and a preoccupied parent can pick up the wrong end of a stick quite easily!

At one stage "Just taking Lindy to Jim" seemed the regular cry as my wife swept down the hall on a Wednesday evening.

"Fine!" I would muster from concentration deep in the study, and all worked well until "Just taking Lindy Tramp Leaning" floated into the study one evening to impinge on the rhythm of things.

What ever happened to Jim?

And whatever they were up to now didn't sound quite nice! Indeed, what help did tramps need in leaning? They seemed inclined to lean quite well anyway. Perhaps leaning was after all not an occupational hazard due to uneven pavements and standing into wind, but rather a nonchalant, cultivated professional stance needing tuition and practice? Or were there special slimming classes for incipient tramps?

And what did a Tramp Leaner actually do? Did the tramp in question need to be inclined to be inclined in the first place? What was in it for the Tramp Leaner? Satisfaction? A job well done? Kudos from leaning thoroughly cantankerous tramps all hours, winter and summer? Was it competitive and did one thus need an approved specification tramp to lean or would any passing tramp still do? And how far, or how many, was the world Tramp Leaning record?

The calm of the study floundered in the torrent of unanswered questions as the front door closed…

"What about Jim, Darling?"

Our daughter's flipped quite off the beam,
Or so it's surely seeming.
At first her passion was for Jim
But now it's for TRAMP LEANING!

We hope it's just a passing craze
A fad done 'when in Rome',
But no! (where DID we go wrong?)
She wants to bring one home!

You can't hush up a thing like that!
The neighbourhood will quack!
But once tramp leaning is passé
I'm sure we'll all bounce back.

Staines 11 12 84

Lindy went on to become a proficient tramp leaner, bought a large one for
the back garden and became a qualified coach, but that's another story for
another time.

Who knows?

Have you noticed that many poems, often very good ones, are written by Anon? Now, who is this modest Anon? Poems don't just pop out of eternity into existence: pouf – voilà! Oh look! There's a new poem draped over there!

Someone is behind them.

Maybe they are written by someone sensitive to criticism who intends to own up after the reviews? Or an Hon. anxious to remain incognito to protect the dignity of his title and office or avoid ridicule in the House? Or An On, a Chinaman quite beyond anyone's power to scrute; or…

But these propositions overlook the time factor. These poems span more than just an era or two, if not an aeon or more.

Furthermore, since a non could not write poems, I am increasingly inclined to the theory that they are all the work of a Nun. Not I feel a regular 'good works' Nun nor an 'evangelical' or a 'contemplative' Nun; nor even a 'prancing, habit flinging, the hills are alive' type Nun.

No. These works are surely by the Sisters of the Secret Scrivening, a very old, self effacing closed order vowed to plenish the world with poems under the classic, impersonal and timeless nom de plume* "A Nun" which indifferent handwriting and ignorant general usage has disguised further as "Anon".

Oh look! There's a brand new poem lying on the next page!

---

* Possibly French Nuns, would you say??

So L o n g !

If
An eon
Got a gee on,
Would it go on
And on
And
On
An'
ON ...
an ....
...
... on
... ?

Anon.*

---

* This poem, I have on authority, was the work of the famous investigator
   Justin Choiring** and not Sisters of the Secret Scrivening at all.
** (A nuther nom de plume.) More of that anon!

Staines 15 11 90

Waving

As a young man in Singapore I had the use of my father's kingfisher blue Morgan+4 sports car. This is just the sort of unusual motor car from which the driver will wave to any other that he may encounter, but since ours was the only Morgan in Singapore I had no motorised waving practice until I drove a Citroën 2CV many years later. Then you could wave your hand through the open roof and do a really good job of it!

Pass by on a train, or under a motorway bridge; sail into or out of a harbour, or along a river, and complete strangers will wave to you. It's a curious compulsion, but for what? What are they achieving?

Are they saying "Oi! This is me. Here I am, over here!" Perhaps, but I doubt this is what royalty are doing from their open topped carriages! They are saying "We see you", acknowledging and relating to the throng that already know where they are. So recognising and being recognised both come into it.

Is waving done to avoid the emptiness of a life alone? Is it affirmation of one's existence? Is it making friends or alliances against future need, or just saying "Hi there! How are you?"

Maybe waving is all of these, but it is interesting to note that we respond to waving more than we understand what it is about. Close your fist and waving takes on quite another meaning! Maybe that's where the message really lies, in the hand itself.

Fellow Man

A dot upon a mountain ridge
Two mile or more away
Immobile but for minutes
It makes its lonely way
Along the edge of Heaven
This heather cloud flecked day.

Now gone, beyond the sky sharp edge,
I scan the razor ridge,
As if I knew the walker,
As if my eye could bridge
The lofty void, o'er fly the stream,
(As only mind's eye can.)
And say to that small dot up there,
"I see you, Fellow Man!"

Brecon Beacons 20 04 92

Endangered Species

Consider Creation. It is quite staggering that so much exists that is so diverse. But then consider extinction! What is it all about? Why evolve something for thousands of millions of years to a subtlety and refinement of boggling intricacy and unique precision only for it to pass away forever the moment the last one dies. The End!

With brave technologies that cannot bring back a single perished cell, let alone an animal, such thoughts dramatise our responsibility. Man has learned how to kill with extravagant variety, but as a conserver or creator he has some way to go.

In London Zoo we carne across the Golden Lion Tamarin, a delightful little marmoset: alert, agile and very appealing. Beside the cage was a notice:

"ENDANGERED SPECIES. ONLY 100 IN THE WILD"

and for comparison the world population in round figures:

6,000,000,000.

The notice did not add "in the wild" but given the way mankind behaves it would seem quite appropriate.

Big Brother

The Golden Lion Tamarin
Is very near extinction.
Just one hundred in the wild
Gives them this distinction.

I stood and pondered this awhile
And calculated thus:-
For every single one of him
There are sixty million us!

London Zoo 28 09 86
Look into their eyes and you might begin to feel uneasy. Sapient eyes
look back; sometimes right through you, staring as if into infinity, or at
extinction.

Two Way Stare

On the whole I like animals, but I'm not so sure it's mutual. I vividly recall as a young lad in India being chosen by a black water-buffalo for chasing. The beast just took umbrage, rose up from its wallowing and thrashed after me like a horned frigate through a typhoon, while I legged it in a zig zag adrenalin haze along the little raised bunds between the paddies.

On a later occasion, in Malaya, something concealed, quick and venomous bit my calf as I stepped over a log. I guess I stood on its tail, disturbed its siesta or otherwise upset it but the result was an erupting Vesuvius of a sore that lasted months and left a 10mm round scar. 'Stand on the log, and step wide' would have kept us apart.

I have had better relations with other animals such as labradors, guinea pigs and red eared terrapins. But feeding, patting, being licked or wetted on lacks dramatic cachet, so no more of them here.

The zoo is my only other exposure to the feral fauna of the world, so far without mishap or trauma, and even at that safe remove my respect runs deep. But it's a two way stare at the zoo. The animals are there because we have power over them. We are there because they have power over us.

Zoo Illogical

I'm not quite sure,
When in the Zoo,
If I am there to see -
Or whether all the animals
Come there to look at me!

So I steel myself
And stare them back,
Unflinchingly, like stone,
Blind to all their antics,
Pretending I'm alone!

I act all anty social,
(The pachyderm's just thick skinned!)
And termites are always boring,
While the camels have the wind.
At reptiles I stare cold blooded,
For the beaver I don't give a dam!
I firmly ignaw all the rodents
And see the wild boar - as ham!

Now the snakes are sometimes a-peeling,
But the fish are decidedly - wet!
The giraffe is orfly superior,
(And that's the view of his Vet.)
I reserve a pinion of the birds,
But I simply must confess,
Whatever I think of the others,
The lions are a roaring success!

For Ross,
London Zoo 29 09 86

Social Climbing

For some reason the first two lines of this poem just ran into my head, waving their incongruity at me until they caught my attention, then demanded to be set down.

The idea that social climbing has its own equipment amused me. To the social climber phrases, accents and notions are his karabiners, crampons and ice axes, with which to secure his grip, reduce the risk of slips or sudden falls, and to speed progress to the pinnacle.

From there the poem just evolved.

Clotted Cream

Pater is a plumber,
And Mater drives a bus.
Sissy is a sales-girl,
How AWF'LLY glamorous!
We boys all went to Eton,
But nearly lost our way -
The place was FULL of tourists
So decided not to stay!

Our Residence ... , (we rent it),
Is set in LOVELY grounds!
The lawns, though RATHER limited
Suffice to run the hounds,
And of a summer evening,
On the terrace, in the cool,
We watch our koi goldfish
Swim round and round the pool.

We also share a pied-a-terre
(Two weeks in southern Spain.)
Which we could swop for elsewhere
'Cross half the world's terrain!
But contemplating Cuba once
Just landed us in strife ...
The distaff members wouldn't fly ...
Instead we drove to Fife.

Our church - (THE C OF ENGLAND!)
We support by stewardship,
Or organising raffles, and
An 'Old Folks' annual trip.
But worship's not our forte
So we go on Christmas Day,
But we LIKE the Vicar socially.
(When he's seldom know to pray!)

Still ...
It's great to HAVE tradition ...
To maintain the upper lip,
In dotty BRITISH fashion;
Its FRIGHTFULLY toodle pip!

Staines 07 02 91

Human Nature

"You can't change Human Nature! It's just a fact: I'm naturally assertive / aggressive / bad tempered / etc.* It's a foible of my character."

How often have you heard this defensive phrase when people feel they need some irrefutable reason for having fallen below an accepted norm. Yet have you also noticed that even those who claim to be liberated and take pride in being independent of society's standards, are curiously hot to use it too!

The truth is, accepted norms do exist and when we transgress we know! Like the rest of mankind I have ducked behind this protective palisade from time to time, but the more often I look at it, the weaker it appears.

And if Human Nature cannot be changed what is education and character building, or even evolution, about? Of course one can change the way one is, it's an act of choice, of will and practice, and the longer we cling to the security of our foibles the slower our own development will be!

Day dreaming ('creative introspection'!) is a little foible of mine and we all know Human Nature can't be changed... Bunkum! Never the less, mild day dreaming and washing up, do seem to be recurring themes in my life. Perhaps with a little more creative introspection I might yet be able to eliminate washing up!

*Choose or insert your own word to taste!

Washed Up Bottle

I watched it bob among the foam
Then visioned up a shore ...
Far, far off. Far off from here,
Where it washed up once more ...
A beach, palm fronds and sun burnt sea,
The kiss of fragrant breeze ...
My message from this distant land ...
What message? If you please!
The bottle's void, not even capped;
Its slowly filling up!
So rinse it in the soapsuds
And finish washing-up!

Staines 18 05 84

Evolutionary Tools

When we visited HMS Victory with our children they were somewhat disappointed. Only half masts existed, without rigging, and the bowsprit and large parts of the bow were altogether missing. HMS Victory looked rather worse for wear then than when she got back from Trafalgar! Now she is restored, and even with modern warships juxtaposed, she looks magnificent.

But these ships and their naval guns point accusingly at us over the ages. Sailing past Victory and her progeny on a cross-Channel ferry I was struck again by the sheer cost of mankind's primitive nature.

Consider the effort: the dock facilities, the ships, the thought and skill, the weapons, aircraft, shells, bullets, mines, torpedoes, missiles, etc. All because we mistrust, or are mistrusted!

Though Neanderthal man is now nattily dressed, he is clearly still at the helm of international problems. But there is hope. Man chose, rather unwittingly perhaps, to use truth, co-operation, insight and change among his evolutionary tools so, while he may have forgotten how to use them, they do still work!*

These tools can also be used by individuals if they choose to set about renovating their otherwise rather creaky Human Nature. When that happens, what a difference it makes to everything!

Now, if I were King…

---

* Having written these lines, August 1991 has come and gone. Much yet needs to be done but is it just possible that some of these old tools may have been rediscovered?

Approximations

Victory, high on dry-dock shores,
(Shorn of motion; airy ocean!)
"Here Nelson Fell"
Is all it says,
Brass plate, without emotion,
"Here Nelson Fell"
Is all it says.
In Portsmouth is the notion!

There is no time or date set down,
No longitude, or platitude!
"Here Nelson Fell"
Is all it says,
In sparsely British attitude.
"Here Nelson Fell"
Is all it says.
It matters not the latitude!

And now this pressing, gangled crew
Stand and pry, then sidle by.
"Here Nelson Fell" Is all it says,
As more move up to spy.
"Here Nelson Fell"
Is all it says.
"Approximately!" Say I!

Staines 16 06 83

Root and Branch

There was once a young husband who disputed boundaries with his neighbour.

Then a child was born and the young father's interest in boundaries waned somewhat as his attentions focussed on his daughter. Truce slowly began to take hold. So all was well.

But soon the child was crawling. Then, as spring came, toddling. The young father thought, "She will need to be safe in the garden" so he mended the fences and fell out with his neighbour.

But for the sour sound of solicitor's letters the summer was sweet. The father showed the girl ants and beetles and butterflies. He showed her plants gradually shooting into flower. He explained what could and could not be eaten and pointed out all that was dangerous in the garden. With earnest instruction he removed all the deadly berries from one bush at the end of the garden as she watched wide eyed. Eventually he was confident the child could play safely in the garden, happy that no harm would befall her. So all was well.

But the child was childish, and in time more poison berries grew. Their bright colours caught her attention and she picked them, to look at. But the brambles against the wall were different, she knew they were safe. It was not long after when her Daddy found her lying very still. All was not well.

In time she recovered and her father began to understand that identifying danger does not remove it. To avoid poison fruit he must deal with the deepest roots of the offending weed. So he dug out the bush and burned it!

About this time the solicitor's efforts were beginning to bear some sour and costly fruit, but as he contemplated the cost he noticed that quite a few of the 'roots' grew on his side of the boundary! He saw hard attitudes and sharp suspicion. He recognised that greed had weighed more than truth, and that he didn't like backing down when wrong!

But recalling the bush, and not without great effort, he dug out the roots on his side and apologised to his neighbour. Silence engulfed the solicitors, but the neighbour also discovered some roots to deal with, and dialogue developed.

As trust grew, it was not long before solicitors, disputes and then even the fences were unnecessary, so they took them down. The little girl now had twice the garden to play in, and a new grandad too! Building on his experiences the young man became a sought after peacemaker. So all was well.

On Old Battlegrounds

Let slip the crowd;
Let still quick time;
Let free the binding mind,
Then listen to the seeping sound
That vapours from the very ground,
The pulse of past mankind.

Sip up the dew;
Soak through the skin;
Sink in the savoured air.
Release the shrieking cannon wreak
And feel red fear in high, and meek
That once fought mortal here.

Remember men;
Read out the rolls;
Record the carnage cost,
For what was then the cause to kill
So shortly shone - yet laid them still,
Scythed like hay upon the hill,
Their Victory too - now lost.

Staines 22 11 91

Effective Revolution

From Newry in Northern Ireland two roads run down to Carlingford Lough, one on each side of the Clanrye River.

Five miles down stream the southern bank of the Clanrye becomes the border with Eire. The place is called Narrow Water for good reason, for the banks pinch together again to what may be less than 100 feet. The castle here suggests that the place has been long known as significant.

We pulled into the car park on the northern bank to enjoy the beautiful tranquillity. Later we learned that a few months earlier this was where soldiers has been ambushed and gunned down from across the water. Implacable bitter men had lurked here resolved to kill.

But what does bitterness ever resolve? Nothing. Bitterness only begets itself, and destroys its begetter first. Nothing can be built from it. It corrodes everything.

World-wide many new, fairer structures and systems are needed, but to date when such social upheaval has been achieved, no great improvement has resulted. Primaeval motives were left unchanged. Result? The same inadequate human mess as before! Mistrust, deadlock, bitterness, bloodshed; round it goes! Restructuring does not touch the real problem. Revolutionary change is needed.

But to be effective revolution must be revolutionary: internal, beginning when you honestly deal with what needs to change in yourself. Primitive 'external' revolution, where guns are pointed and everyone else does the changing and you cling to stone age righteousness, is just naive and reactionary! Anyone can see it won't work! It inflames, sets a bitter example, and surprise surprise, people just resist – then round it goes again!

Parked Cars

Two parked cars,
Empty by the fence rail,
Overlooking Narrow Water,
Nudge the beams,
Quiet as monuments
This calm afternoon.

Yet grief has wrung
It's full toll from this spot.
Here raw hate has blazed
For blood and revenge,
Tearing young men apart!

Right here ...
Silent as graves
Stand two parked cars
At Warrenpoint,
Marking the spot.

Dundalk 12 08 84

Behind Montreux

A funicular railway* climbs 5,500ft, steeply up behind Montreux, Switzerland, stopping at villages perched on protruding knees or in draped valleys far above. The last stop delivers passengers to the Rochers de Naye (6,699ft), right at the top. From here the view is panoramic and breathtaking, with the French Alps opposite and the Upper Rhone valley to the left, and the Dents du Midi to one side. Geneva is not visible but Lake Geneva lies silvery, curving under the mountain skirts to the right.

You can descend by train, or walk down, or eagle it out over the sheer edge in a hang glider more than a mile above the lake.

Switzerland leaves you in no doubt: when you are up, you are up, and when you are down, you are down! But when you are only half way up you are at Caux, on this particular funicular!

By the station stands Mountain House, totally impressive – for it was one of the great hotels, a watering place for the aristocracy at the end of the Belle Epoch, and it looks it. It is now used as a gracious conference centre addressing the essential needs of individuals and nations.

It was from a room in Mountain House looking west down the length of the lake that I watched God whip up a furious storm and hurl it against the mountain from perhaps twenty miles away. It raged for only a few minutes before all was quite calm again, but it left a strong impression of just how powerless and puny we really are.

* Interestingly, the locals don't regard walking up the mountain as at all eccentric, indeed on Swiss National Day brass bands stride up the mountain, playing lustily the while, to waken people.

Let There Be Storm

"Let there be storm!"

God said.

"Let there be rock-torn wind!
Let lightning thunder round!
Let shriek the grappling sky!
Let sky with sea compound!
Let wind prick, sharp with rain!
Let wince the spattled ground!
And by this, let Man see My
Power - and Love abound!"

Said God.

And so saying,
Strode He in thunderous steps
To scribe this mystery round
And saw He; it was right,
For sea and sky and ground.

And then there was storm,
Sparking at His feet
As He swept the cloudy hem
Of His mighty cloak about Him.

Caux 19 08 86

Together

She winked at me. At three years and ten months, over her boiled egg, she winked at me. "Look Daddy, I can wink one eye closed!" and with the complete rearrangement of her face, she could.

Everything stopped as I joined in. The egg spoon poised in her concentrating fist, itself half high. Every muscle and sinew, every thought and thrill, hers and mine, focussed on the closing of an eye against the opening of the other, and she winked!

Both of us were drained happy. We had willed, and it had worked. The effort of achievement, the less than dramatic yet more than important moment flooded us together those few instants and we laughed, delighted in our private conspiracy. She winked at me. Where do we go from here?

Happily, she grew up. But we still share delicious moments like the occasion when a film opened with a strong location shot of Tower Bridge. We turned to each other, nodded, and in unison said: "New York!" We collapsed laughing. That shared zany moment kept us chuckling for quite a while.

Such things are bridges between the age groups and give meaning and fun to growing up and growing older. Without those interage bridges of open unguardedness anyone can get lost, stuck at a stage and look for 'meaning' in some disastrous places. You have all seen them.

Poppy Days

Somehow he never grew up;
Fifteen kidnapped him in passing.
Now, the new crowd ignore him,
Despite his gyrations,
And studied oblivion;
'Gone' with the megawatted jazz.

Yet see him,
This dated flower person,
Escaping. 'Gone',
With eyes tight shut
Behind the old badge
Of steel rimmed cycle round specs,
Eager to be appreciated
For his 'hip'.

But, for all the beat,
The power at his feet
Swings his torpid limbs
Shy of the tempo; and he sways;
Blown as a poppy,
Un-coordinated;
Thick with intent.

And poppy red,
Swathed in poppy-red flying shirt,
Sheened and creased,
Loose as the poppy petal
He stomps.
And his pate,
Nestling, as the poppy head,
Among the shock stamens
Of his dark hair,
Seems to be as hollow
And as full of smokey dreams,
As he sniffs
To keep away the ache
Of silence and reality.

Yet it means nothing,
This flower power trip.
It is blotting paper
For the dribble of pain
Felt for something promised
And beyond recall;
For the dead dreams.
For the laudanum days.
For the celibacy
Of an endless childhood.

Blackburn, Buckie 12 08 85

On the Prom

I am lucky to have married my best friend and it is always a pleasure to catch up with what she has been doing when we have been apart awhile.

A conference in Brighton had taken Sheila away for a few days and the children and I drove down to meet her at the end. It was a stunning day and Brighton was brim full of people, spilling out of the town onto the beach and into the sea.

The poem was a challenge. There was much to see and say about the day and I wanted to catch the moving kaleidoscope of events on the Front, as it happened, in one slow observation. It would be a long poem.

In the end it pleased me, but I'm biased. I guess the acid test is whether you are drawn into the occasion and on to the end!

Brighton

It was a reunion,
And the four slim days had folded
Onto the reams and stack of experience,
Like the cards that cue
Some huge Hurdy Gurdy.

There was much to unfold and feel.
So we talked and walked, fingers fitted,
Rapt in our exchanges,
While the children swept,
Like gulls in the sun
Calling and wheeling,
Happy, about the flanks
Of our conversation,
As we dawdled by
Darning the small rent.
So we were blind, save for insight,
Oblivious, steered as if by radar,
Through the flock and throng
That peopled the promenade.

Perhaps it was our children,
Keen eyed and eager seizing opportunity,
Who steered us, who gently tugged
And berthed us safe, seated
On a wall beside the paddling pool!

And there we sat
Full three half hours,
Restful as two barges
Gently gunwaling each other —
Growing slowly silent,
The urgent ideas ebbing
In the tongue stilling sun.

Then sight returned.
Unperceived, mousy as morning.
Seeping, spilling, gushing,

Until the din of day-wake
Ransacked our reflections
And thrust consciousness
Back into the cannonade of light.

Activity saturated the engulfing day
Drenching us with interest.
It broke over our rock-stillness
And shoaled about us!

The day was as fish full
As the dimpled sea
That buttered up the beach
In little ripples
Which, far out,
Had rocked the RESCUE boat,
Adrift on that other world.

It's plain from here that he's bored.
Like his boat,
The lolling lifesaver's mind drifts,
Afloat on shore-thoughts,
No doubt anchored
In 'The Anchor'
Or on some back seat.
Again, he sweeps his salt limbs
Admiring the tanned manliness,
Lonely and incongruous
In the carmine dayglo bathing cap.
Unfulfilled. Un-needed.
A 'municipal precaution'
Urgently in need of action.

His dreams float up a maiden,
Sea ready, full as a gooseberry,
And without ceremony
He damsels her into difficulties
So that he, his boat, his all, may respond,
Plunging to her rescue and then ... !
A gliding gull un-girls him,

Bombing his dreamboat,
Athwartships.

Turn now from the red lettered boat
And notice nearby,
Within the hum of humanity,
A sort of silence growing;
A lower hush, a tonal shift.
The men are falling silent,
Admiring in waves
The bronzy belle
Blazing by in the sun,
And precious little else!
Nonchalant she strolls,
This real life lifesaver's love.
Conscious in every pore
Of the yearn and stare-wash she leaves,

She cleaves her course,
Breasting the silent heaving sighs
Under her tiny, tight reefed,
Burst to breaking, bikini sails.
And her hull hips ship roll slow;
Oceanic, way beyond the horizons
Of their hope,
Or chance, or opportunity.

And all the while
The romp and roar
Of wet pool warmed children
High registers around,
Until she is lost to sight
And sound abounds again.

Then, in ones and twos,
Among the naked babes
And pale, pimple flanks
Of the Saturday sun seekers,
Comes a Carribean crowd.
Smooth skinned ebony families,

Lads, pin polished on parade.
Ribbanded girls, frilled, pretty,
Each in full blown bloom,
High hued, extravagant,
Against their dark ground.

And in their carefree passing
Was none of English reticence.
Theirs was joy and freedom,
Goodwill gospelling
From every seam and step,
Louder than their convention badges.
Their bearing broadcast their Faith,
Our God. Alive!

But where was God some sixty seasons past,
When this skew man was made?
What slip, or purpose,
Breathed him so
To gaunt ghost his life away,
Caught crooked
In his own skeletal claw;
Unable to escape the stare pity,
Or petty sympathy, or recoil.

But his royalty is real.
For though he treads with burdened care,
Who of us could raise his smile
To trade it for our stare?
And I too stare, ashamed,
Transfixed by the skewer of his hump,
From which he seems to hang,
Walking dangled,
But just upon the ground.

See too his head
Lantern slung,
Hung loosely forward
To part the grey stream
Of the curtaining coat
Cascading from his shoulders,
Frozen in the sun.

And there, beyond the grey margins,
The scrawny space within, revealed
For others' stares to pry
The working of his walking.
So, in royal solitude he goes,
Reviewing the dumb Guard of Honour
That forms and reforms
Whichever way he faces.

We stirred, and shared a word,
As palmy islands share a breeze.
Content, lulled and lapped warm,
Washed by time, and senses so little used
In the crash and tide
Of yesterday and tomorrow.
And the day, and play of people goes by.

Now, hot pottering poolward
Patters a curly headed girl,
Eve simple entirely
In her second summer.
She straightens course
Past our promontory,
Soaked in thoughts of water play,
With determined elbows swinging
To the drum tumble of her tread,
And chance glances up,
Shy, sideways,
And meets my eyeing smile,
Then flashes back her own.

It was an instant. Over!
Then she passed behind my love,
And I, worldly,
Never moved my head to see her again.
But she ... she was stabbed and thrilled!
Romance, for a moment writhed within her,
Tugging her resolution round
Into the shade we made,
To risk another encounter!

Then by my side I heard 'Hello',
And turned to see her wheel
Upon her heel
As she faltered and fled,
Once more pulled
By the cool and raucous pool;
Her first and only
Really magnetic true love
This innocent afternoon.

But here's a sight!
Some aged Americenne
High heels by,
Gripping fast the past
In her skimpy summer jib
And slack shorts.

Mature discretion
Would have clad sparse spars
In graceful mainsails
And T'gallants,
But instead ...
'Thar she blows!'
All stringy rigging
On thin bare poles
Quite unreasonably brown.
You have to laugh.

And laugh they do.
As one jaded Judy
Struts off to deliver
Her remaining punch
Another, older Punch
Enthralls, and mauls
Another faded Judy,
Intently, by the wall,
Sweaty in the candystripes.

The small show now held a crowd
Where age was no distinction
For all were involved,
Meshed into each detail and twist
Of the tiny tale
Portraying their common humanity.

Gradually each guarded foible,
Each raw emotion,
Stripped of manners and control,
Appears as jest
To polarise the parable.
And young and old saw equally
The meaning of this comedy
And the louder laughed
As if shouting scorn
At the day-lit face
Of such rebellion!

And still we sat,
Bookless bookends on a shelf.
As much the audience
To this small show
As we were props
In the grander play
The puppets parodied.

Then there was an end.
Just as endless afternoon
Marks itself off from evening,
There was an end.

And the next beginning,
Quiet, yet certain as any cue
Beckoning us back on stage
To act out our weekly lines,
Fresh each day
To each new audience.

Staines 06 09 82

Large Neighbourhood

Tirley Garth is an extraordinary place. The big house stands impressive on a tablecloth of trim lawn among formal gardens and forty acres of landscaped Cheshire hill side.

In spring the gardens blaze with daffodils, azaleas and rhododendrons. In summer the gardens fill with fruit and flowers, mature and generous. In autumn and winter: rolling, open, tranquil.

But what makes Tirley quite extraordinary is that it is valued and visited by neighbours from twelve thousand miles around, who forge there workable personal, national and even international ideas for the future. A very stimulating place.

Tirley has numerous formal and two informal ponds. This poem was written about one of the lower ones. I had gone there to reflect in peace, shaded by the foliage, one still summer afternoon.

By Tirley Pond

Among the stalks,
Among the tall green handles
Of the up-blown umbrella foliage,
Stalks a moorhen chick,
Pulling herself through
The deep leaf, pond edge, green shade,
A peck at a time.
A downy dot of deeper dark
Intent on expedition and concealment,
Not even dimpling the reflections,
Like the rising fish.

And above the pond
A dainty air raid
As gnats combat,
While delicate damsel fly
Tandem-hover in,
Air lifting their eggs, precisely,
Risking life, or sudden oblivion,
On ancient changeless orders,
Known also to the fish.

Now a steady lash of ripples
Flow from the far shore into view.
Left, right goes the lifted head
As if undecided.
But the snake swam straight,
Across the pond towards me,
Certain of its solitude,
Cool bellying the pond-weed
In the sun.

But the sudden sight
Of this sure swimming snake
Feinting towards me
Triggered the trap
Of Adam's Eden old fear,
So that I sprang up,

As much in defiance as in dread
Of this sure swimming, oncoming head.
And in the sunshine we both froze
And eyed the minutes past
In unswerving obedience
To our archetypes.

Then I moved away,
For it was his pond
Not mine.

Staines 22 06 83

Singapore Salad Days

One of the great and oft repeated weekend options when I lived in Singapore aged twenty, was to gather a group of friends (never too hard if one put the word about the Swimming Club), and with a large picnic and a crate of beer, head off early to Jardine Steps in Kepple Harbour to hire a small motor sampan and boatman for the day.

The voyage out to one of the many tropical islands just to the south was only a matter of an hour or so. Some islands are small enough to walk round in ten minutes, others would take two or three hours. Some, for their broader beach, their better view, or deeper shade were more favoured than others but all without exception were truly beautiful places with lush vegetation, spotless sand, and water that gave the sense of swimming in light white wine.

Each island had a vigorous ringing reef shot through with fish, crabs, anemones, kelps and much else. But even paradise is flawed and we each swam with a stick to scoop up free-swimming banded sea snakes and hoist the hapless creatures far out to sea!

Once the picnic and beer were ashore and a shady camp had been set up above the jetsam line people would make for the bushes to emerge in their bathing costumes. This intention could also be frustrated, for there are coral-red ants about half an inch long that colonise foliage here and they are called Fire Ants for good reason! Pick your changing bush too hastily in an effort to get swimming first, and you could come dancing back onto the beach moments later, quite oblivious of your state of attire, flailing and wailing in an effort to sweep the aggressive little fellows away. Quite hilarious to watch!

In the water, you entered another world. The play of sunlight split by the rocking sea surface patterned the dense coral beds just a few feet below the belly with constant movement. Bright fish lurked in nooks or darted about their business often cocking a wary eye as they slid away, listed over to look up at you. Mobile molluscs mooched along munching algae, while others fanned their insides with food by gentle pulsation.

At the seaward edge the reef rim rose higher and life was even more intense. The outer reef edge sloped away very steeply, a sheer wall down into the gradually dimmer depths until the mysterious ocean drew its veil over further revelation. Mostly we would swim and dive over the inner reef for it was beautiful, bounteous and safe. But youth is drawn to excitement and occasionally we would swim to the rim, and on a lung-full dive swift and deep down the darkening wall, to test our stamina and nerve.

Down over the edge there was a current and it was noticeably colder, which added strongly to the feeling of being on someone else's patch. A sheer wall on one side and dark water beside and below made one feel very obvious, aware that many of the native denizens are large, limber and able to see you well before you see them!

We could not linger on a lung-full, so at about 25, perhaps 30, feet we would turn and propel ourselves to the surface, emerging like super-charged corks before our lungs gave out. From below, the surface always looked so reassuring. Our own world: light, air and friends seen far above the fronds, corals and bursts of fishes, all silhouetted against the clouds and sky.

On one occasion two other lads and I decided we would bivouac overnight on the beach under a blanket suspended against some rocks. The others would come back the next day for us. That evening was magical. We sat and talked and drank beer, made our sand scrapes comfortable and about midnight set about sleeping. But the wind, light as it was at ground level was carrying quite a lot of fine dry sand!

After some experimenting we erected a foot high windward barrier of ant free twigs and leaves. This little hedge did the trick. It slowed the wind which dropped the sand and in the morning we had quite a little dune, but the hedge offered us another far from anticipated comfort.

At about two o'clock the slow-ahead of a quiet marine engine stirred our skimpy sleep and we peered from under our plaid rug roof across the moonlit beach. A thirty foot launch without lights of any kind was stealing round the end of our island on the rising tide. It hove to about seventy five yards from us and shut down engines. Various figures launched a rubber dinghy into which two men climbed and quietly rowed ashore.

By now the three of us were not happy and very wide awake! We were a long way from home, not far from Indonesian territory, and in the middle of the night. Smuggling was a major and well publicised local pastime but shortsighted youth had not contemplated this when the plan to stay over was so readily undertaken!

The men moved off, thankfully toward the opposite headland, then stopped and spent twenty minutes quartering that piece of beach. They then moved round the headland and out of sight. Time passed, but our straining eyes and ears could only detect the boat and the empty beach. An hour went by, then another. Our eyes grew sore with staring into the moonlight through our camouflage of twigs and leaves!

Eventually the men reappeared, behind us! Coming round a bluff of rocks barely thirty feet away, each carrying something, they passed within three feet of our seaward screen, making for the dinghy! If they didn't hear my heart, they were either deaf or it had stopped! A soft whistle, engines coughed, the dinghy went quietly out and the launch slid darkly away.

Who were they? What were they doing? What would our presence have meant to them? By now, drained, sleepless but very relieved, we were exhausted and our friends could not believe we were still fast asleep when they arrived mid morning!

Salad days! Many afternoons passed sunning, swimming and talking about being newly adult, playing silly beach games, showing off, tossing the driftwood caber, crawling races, mapping one's life, watching tropical sunsets and sparkling phosphorescent waves lap the sand or stream from the sampan prow on the cool, bucking night rides back to Jardine Steps, with salty, sun-caked skin.

There is so much of mystery, beauty and fearful respect in water. Its images, from without and within are very varied and powerful and its constant appeal seems to hark us back to an earlier time, when the element was perhaps not quite so foreign to us.

Even a pond draws one's attention, evoking utterly different wonder and response than the tropical ocean.

By the Top Pond

Sentinel, the trees crowd by
This leaf locked silent pond
And wrestle with the eager breeze
To keep the calm within profound.

But day-long does the nimble wind
Slip past the guardian grove,
To riffle leaf hung skirting limbs
That grace the pond with gentle bows.

Then a wind-run cloud pulls free
And swords of sunlight, plunging strike!
Yet nothing stirs. The pond is still
A green-brown skin; a sky
With clouds of lily leaves thereon.

Reflections pulse on rippled rings
That jostle to the shore
While the casual fish drift round,
Staring, stupid and pond bound.
A gang, idling the afternoon,
 Vandalising lilies,
Sucking on the surface, like a fag.

One tiny island floats, adrift,
Awash with nettles overall.
Moored by roots, it longs
In skyward leaning,
To acknowledge the sun,
While all else is drawn in, by the pond.

Then Night, black pond rot
Night Queens the stirsome wind to quit
And in her slow embrace she turns
This bird-freed fief into another realm.
Dead leaves now cloud the floating moon
And stars upon the leaden waters weep
Their silent ripples from the sky.

Tirley 02 09 91

In Laws

There was a time when I had a brother-in-law, in Law. He was and is a pharmacist. Later he moved from the village of Law and became a lawyer. Had he stayed he would have been my brother-in-law, in Law, in Law!

I have several mostly-medical in-laws, and this poem is for one of them, my much loved little sister-in-law, in-tently in-volved in surgery, in Australia.

She went to Australia seeking to increase her experience. Surgically I cannot comment, but if marriage counts, she certainly succeeded!

When this poem was written she anticipated being away for a year, but she settled. So now everyone has a grand excuse for visiting her in Oz, and they duz!

Airlines

World: Small world!
Hemispheres unfurled!
Hong Kong ere long;
Catchee Chinee sing song ...
"Silky shirt?
Cheap's dirt!"
Cards to friends,
From the ends
Of the Earth ...

On! Jet on!
Time zones gone.
Melbourne next morn.
New experience. New dawn.
Work. Play.
Year away.
Leave friends At the ends
Of the Earth ...

Home! Sweet home!
Bombay, Dubai, Rome,
Heathrow, Glasgow.
Old friends. Go slow.
Torrent talks.
Linn Park walks
With a friend;
At the end,
That's its worth ...

Staines 20 07 85
For Tricia with much love and a little envy!

Left at Pretty Pine

I want to take you to a landscape so flat that they laser level it to find any 'high' point from which to flow their irrigation schemes to water rice fields. This is southern New South Wales.

We drove up from Melbourne to Echuca on the big brown Murray River, crossed into New South Wales and on to Deniliquin. The directions then said "left at Pretty Pine, left again to Algonquin".

We arrived at dead of night at an old, tin topped, dusty and flaking wooden bungalow that looked as if it had just been caught brawling. Now it leaned exhausted staring into our headlights. We let ourselves in, stepping over the out-board motor, a 22 rifle, a scattered assortment of towels, picnic bags, and bits of this and that. In another room we found a large loose-jointed wooden bed with an unyeilding mattress that resembled the topography of the Hindu Kush. We filled our sleeping bags and slept.

Next day we crossed a levee into one of the few remaining vestiges of virgin gum forest, and on down to the so-slow Edwards River, an offshoot and then tributary of the Murray. Two Emus paced away as our car approached. When we stopped, an aboriginal quiet hung everywhere, like the peeling gum bark.

The moment was brief. Once out of the car, squadrons of voracious tanker mosquitoes whined steadily at us from the foliage to refuel! We yelled, cursed, slapped and spun. This fandango roused the sulphur crested cockatoos in the gum tops who, unsure of the issues, rooted all out for both sides of the scrap in their scrap-iron rending way! Next day we resembled hot, pink chesterfields!

Later, itching, but far from aerial assault, I sat on some logs behind the dishevelled shack and just looked at the open scene...

.

New South Wales Morning

Grey green tussocks
Bleat downwind
As the mile-away sheep
Move among the Gum stems.
And the sun strikes even
Over the whole scene.

The sky flies hot above,
Rich blue, hueing down
To the baked horizon,
Pale as a white Forget-Me-Not.
Only a scratch of cloud exists,
Coming up from the far side
Of the world.
Stretched beyond the etched
Olive ilex Gums,
At the edge of sight.

Overhead a slow crow flies,
Complaining as he goes
In a crude stage whisper.

And patterned overall,
On the bleach-baked and hard,
Dismembered bones of Gums,
White in the sun,
The beautiful rilling,
Of the bark boring beetle,
Which likely killed them!

All this, spread about,
Out back the shack
Stacked about with wood
And rusty junk of ages,
Accumulating in the sun.
The serenade of grasshoppers
And the soft wind chime
Of Gum leaves.

'Algonquin', Deniliquin NSW 08 05 87

An Old Coinage

Knowledge has been encouraged to run amok, to fulminate everywhere, and we no longer clearly know what shape it's in, nor can we even sketch the broad outlines of the beast.

So now we butcher knowledge for consumption, splitting it first into two crude sides, science and art. From these are trimmed the main cuts, which are sliced again into manageable amounts. Finally bite sized bits are carved off for digestion by individuals. But can the chewer still relate the bite to the beast? Not easily.

Seen another way students in their early teens may choose science or art and leave the other behind confident that it does not and will not matter. So they head on for higher education and degrees.

Eventually, when they have thoroughly digested their chosen portion, they may feel full, well educated, expert. Perhaps so, but expert about so little that the value of their views may not extend much beyond their disembodied speciality.

But 3D Real Life requires more than facts, or techniques. Narrowness is dangerous. It can make another viewpoint or value system invisible! Then experts let us down, and common sense seems uncommon scarce! Oh! for more intelligent generalists!

For a century or so, knowledge has been the coveted coinage while wisdom, the garnered harvest of all that humanises us, now seems folksey, a coloured-bead currency, without purchase power in the market places of life.

Yet it is wisdom that illuminates and guides, and it comes through evaluating and trusting feelings, not data, for insights and truth are borne in on you when deep new understanding dawns through awareness, in silence.

Daughter, 10

The quiet grey light stole softly
Past the parted Sunday morning curtains
And lay gentle, as gentle as moonlight,
Quilting the broad bed where I lay.
My thoughts were wrapt in prayer,
Moving mazily among the needs and cares
Of life when, light and firm she strode
Between the sheets of my mind.

I lay propped, a knee raised
Beside the sprawled and fallen other,
And she climbed up beside me,
Silent, confident, impelled,
Then curled and crooked herself,
Foetal, back towards me on the covers,
And lay her head into the fold
Of my belly and thigh - and was still.

Sun and moons moved and spun - perhaps.
But we lay still,
My arm arching her waist
And hand rested on her hip.

Nothing moved or was said.
Nothing was done:
Only breathing and feeling.
Yet everything was done and said,
And we were moved.

Then, as lightly, it was past.
And she rose and departed
With a feminine fluidity and grace
That swung her hair.
And the soft sip of an air blown kiss
Was all that was ever said.

Staines 04 07 82

A Pretty Neat Trick

My father, seeing a garage grease monkey's prospects as limited, decided to train as an aero engineer. Night school and an apprenticeship did the trick and he achieved his 'tickets'.

He learned to fly as engineer to the Perak Flying Club in Malaya, flew through the war then went back to Malaya with the Dept. of Civil Aviation and rose to be number two.

Meanwhile he kept his engineering tickets up to date, and added the Airline Transport Pilot and Flight Navigator licences to his flying qualifications. With nothing left to sit he resigned his desk job, joined an airline, got his command and thoroughly enjoyed every minute. He straddled all aspects of aviation with deep knowledge, great ability and quiet tact.

At sixteen I spent the long summer holiday in Singapore and as Chief Flying Instructor of the Royal Singapore Flying Club he taught me to fly. From Kallang Airport we went up round and down almost daily between 0600 to 0700, before he went off to work.

He knew me well and expected perfection. I was not allowed mental or mechanical sloppiness in any particular, be it navigating, descending, turning, or simply taxiing. He wanted accuracy at all times and through it he gave me my love and respect for professionalism and precision.

It was a heady experience! I cannot thank him enough, for though I could not hold a power licence I've spent many happy years as a glider pilot where accurate flying makes a great difference!

I rejoined my father at eighteen and spent a year working in a hanger under his direction helping to rebuild a Miles Gemini, a light wooden twin, which he had flown out some years earlier from Britain. Again I learned so much: the use of machine tools, the appreciation of structure, techniques, fitting. All have served me well in other spheres since then. We flew the Gemini with great pride, but wood and casein glue are not 'tropical' and it was sold.

Even today, knowing something about flight and aircraft, I still look up at a 747 or Concord and think "That's a pretty neat trick!". But mechanical flight is just imitation. Even the crane fly, for all it's ungainliness, is a true aviator, while I'm only an envious admirer.

Unconvincing Aviator

See how the Crane Fly
Holds it's legs in flight:
Out stretched to the four winds
Like one blindfolded,
Eager to sense surroundings
That perhaps he cannot see.

Even his flight is hesitant,
Lacking confidence,
Lest he become entangled
In this wilderness
Of wild flowers and grass.

On the whole
An unconvincing aviator!
Insufficient power,
And too much drag,
With an umbrella frame
Undercarriage!

But I bet he tastes good
To the trout!

Wellbrook, Tyrone 20 08 84

Opinion Formers

Say "ideology" and you are likely to have an audience with goose pimples! It reeks of brain washing, manipulation, and servitude and we shudder, glad to be free of all that. But, the 'Age of Ideology' is now! We are daily drenched by ideas competing hard for our attention, support or allegiance; modern communications and advertising have seen to that. Spend more! Think this! Do that!

But we are seldom worried. It seems that this tide of ideas is not aimed at carrying us here or there, it is just informing or prompting us.

It is however subtler than that. The phrase 'opinion formers' gives the clue. Opinions can be and are being formed in accordance with someone else's motives and objectives. This way, we choose apparently freely, quite unaware that the choice may have been rigged!

So why all the slight of hand? It's because ideas are invisible. You can have them privately and they cannot be dislodged by anything except another idea that you regard as 'better'.

If one's basic truths are a bit unformed it is easy to be carried here or there, but not so when one has laid down some fundamental truths by which to steer choices.

Wisdom offers impartial and valuable truth about what is good for us, but in any case, look deep: what motivates? Is it wholesome? Is it good? Where does it lead, up or down?

Being prepared to be bone honest with yourself and to lay foundations only on moral and spiritual bedrock, enables evaluation against those values. When 'better' ideas come along you can make sure that they raise your standards before accepting them! This way people break free, avoid behaving like midges driven by circumstances or other peoples aims.

Midges Maybe

Small flies; midges maybe,
Jostle and flirt in furious haste,
As if to some manic music.
Silent yet imperative
It passions them to fan this
Pollen heady afternoon
To hurricane force,
Turning this peaceful,
Stone mounded stream
Into an Atlantic in miniature.

Now the tempo changes.
The baton of a breeze
Moderates their measure
To a not quite stately bob,
And for a beat all seems appropriate
To this graceful afternoon.

Then the terror sweeps them,
And they frenzy to and fro,
Far too fast for the eye to catch,
Driven by the silent music,
Tyrannied by time,
Surging their symphony of life
Into this one
Short,
Summer sun,
Dancing day.

North Bovey 02 06 82

In Tollymore Park

Tollymore Forest Park on the north east flank of the Mourne Mountains is a lovely place through which gambols at least one busy rivulet.

Too small to retain a name when reduced by 250,000 times on my map, so I cannot be more specific, however at one point this one runs in a shady little curving canyon between sheer rocky walls overhung with wispy vegetation. A robust stone bridge gives views down the few feet to the bed, and of a stony beach on the inside of the curve.

Having by then walked quite a bit, the notion of sitting a while drew me down from the bridge onto the beach where just round the corner, out of sight, I sat attentive on a rock while the others went energetically on.

They came back about an hour later, halloo'd from the bridge and I rejoined them, but not before I had jotted these lines, watching the hero of this poem showing-off in the guy wire sunbeams that seemed to tether the leaf canopy to the ground.

Dragonfly

This cleft of rock is my Kingdom,
This stream, my river of life.
As egg and nymph
I've seasoned here,
In flood and summer,
Year by Year,
And now, on the wing
I'm tyrant here!
Dragonfly, raptor; King!

As nymph I stalked and I plundered;
I gorged on the small and the weak.
With jaws drawn back
I've pillaged here,
Grabbing and crushing,
Striking fear ...
And now, on the wing
I have no peer!
Dragonfly, raptor; King!

Now as I ride on thrilling wings
With thrumming thorax and glide,
I see my prey
And with a beat
I fly him down
And grab my meat,
With a beat of my papery wing;
And all my prey is fearful sweet!
Dragonfly, raptor; King!

Dundalk 13 08 84

A Level Deeper

Life's problems are usually enough, people seldom need more. They hear about other situations and commiserate, but don't or can't identify or perhaps afford to get involved; 'sufficient unto their day is the evil thereof' already. Events are either personal or remote, depending on whether they impinge on one or not.

So the words 'heart-felt' have a special meaning. Information has gone a level deeper than mere head-felt knowing, insight has operated. The hearer has slipped into the other's shoes for long enough to understand, or be touched by compassion. Things heart-felt result in action.

Britain in 1991 saw many people suffering from economic recession. My need for bypass surgery added to our general travail and the news was heart-felt by my sister in law. Her thought was to forego buying new clothes, her passion, until she had saved my fare to join her family in Australia to recuperate!

My news touched her, and went a level deeper. She shared my situation and gave of herself. Needless to say I was very moved and as a thank you wrote 'Heart-Felt' for her.

Heart-Felt

How safe the lordly Lion is
When pacing in a pen,
And how we hope with interest
To hear him roar again.
How smug we are observing,
How quick we are to quip
About our caring attitude:
To let our prattle slip.

But bend the bars and enter!
Now joke within the den,
And note with clammy interest
Your attitudes again!
For now the lordly Lion
And you must interact!
For everyone in person
Must face their fate, as fact.

But when another ventures
To wear another's shoes
And show with caring interest
That the other's news
Is not remote, but heart-felt
The greatest gift is given
For love has then been manifest,
And wrought a bit of Heaven.

Staines 07 06 91

Physical Inflation

The removal men cast a seasoned eye around the five room house we had lived in for fourteen years and confidently concurred on the size of van they would need. Came the day, the only van available was 50% larger, "at no extra", and a good job too! We filled it and our car tight to the crevices!

Our well behaved chattels simply surged out of cupboards and drawers, gulped fresh air, expanded several-fold, and annexed all available space! By midday, as the van departed, the rain set in; not heavy, just a drizzle, but steady and assured, confident of abundant reserves.

Unloading took all afternoon. Our newly expanded possessions now had nine rooms on three floors to fill, and did so without demur! It was tiring work. Then, whilst carrying a small crate, was when the rain, the ramp of the van, and fatigue conspired against me.

Falling in the Rain

There are moments,
Ambered rain drops
From monsooning time,
Microbed through with sensations,
Each a millisecond, intimate,
Before the micro-scan
Of your arrested mind.

There are moments
When your senses yell,
And attention locks,
Laserly, on the drop.
There are moments
When the slight slope
And rainshine
Slip your footfall
That shifted inch
From beneath your mass ...
And down it goes
With a speed visibly slow;
Flailing for balance,
Failing and falling.
Uncontrollably fast!

There are moments
When the very viscera feel loose ...
CRASH! - is so descriptive!
The word would bare its meaning
Wherever it were heard.
Then comes the pain.
Diffused at first,
For the mind has, in a moment,
Barricaded itself,
Surrendering only
To the seiging pain
By graded stages.

Now senses slowly sear!
Sight sees sound - Rag-dolly crunch!
Touch hears contortion
As joints and bones bend
Against their limits.
Smell tastes sick, and blood, and bile
While, against the jaw line
Taste registers dry, rattling pain!

Windless you wait ...
Aware again of the rain
Trickling your face. Moanless you mouth ...
For breath that will not return
For fear of tearing you in half.

There are moments when time -
s.s .. s ... Stops!

North Bovey 24 12 83

Predation -v- Symbiosis

Making a living, or "where's the next meal coming from?" is one of life's great themes. In exchange for constant feeding and tending, the queen bee foregoes all else and specialises. She becomes incapable of anything other than laying eggs, wholly dependent and completely depended upon: symbiosis.

Predators use a different ploy. They make a living persuading things, invariably against their wills, to be eaten. It's a simple scheme, but to succeed they need to be persuasively strong, or irresistible in some other way. Sticky silk for instance, makes many spiders quite irresistible and very effective predators!

But I am attracted by the potentials of symbiosis. It seems more evolved and appeals to my deep sense that we are meant to get along, to co-operate, to assist, and in so doing enjoy both the action and the outcome. Predation is by contrast selfish and primitive, only concerned for its own needs. Nothing else impinges to disturb this egocentric quest.

Selfishness and brawn characterise predation while symbiosis demonstrates integration of abilities for the greater good. The weak and inoffensive can participate, the strong can protect, the clever can help and the much gifted may give freely without fear of pillage. It enables the whole to be a common-wealth at all levels of ability.

Qualifications are useful for earning a living, but bestowed on a predator they do little good to the society that awards them. In the hands of a symbiotic soul, one with the vision to see qualifications as his offering to society, the common-wealth begins to emerge and his own happiness is nigh guaranteed. Symbiosis, each with the other and all with the environment there lies the Evolutionary Path.

Receiver

Sensitive receiver;
Filaments shimmering,
Swaying,
Taut,
As the light
And the breath
Get caught!
Aerial dish.
Receiver
For the arachnid
Gastronomer.

Wellbrook, Tyrone 20 08 84

Procreation

Procreation is a pertinacious business. Just look around! The world is full, far beyond seeming need, with fecundity. Why? The answer is obvious at one level, but such urgency and investment! Why indeed?

If procreation was a mere process set off by circumstances to keep a balance of Nature's numbers, and death simply scrapping life's components for re-use, then life would be finite, pointless, cyclic, going nowhere. Nor would urgency or fecundity be much called for.

Yet life itself senses transience and future, and knows that 'now' is not all, for while we claim foresight for ourselves and some of the 'higher orders', even algae reproduce!

Life behaves like an eager, pervasive force, an Entity, aware within itself of its diversity and its destiny. Now, if death is an omnivorous counter force out to succeed, and not just Nature's Cleansing Department, reproductive urgency and excess is clearly a competitive necessity! But death could not lose if life was finite, and what would it matter anyway, if life had no point?

Only if life is not competing, if death has no dominion but, like a catalyst, transforms life from physical to spiritual, does the matter begin to make sense. Procreation is about generation not maintenance – new life for its own sake – with urgency and fecundity suggesting the very Universe may depend on it! Who knows, it may.

Whatever life is and however it works, procreation is a priority subject, and all living thing take a keen interest in all that pertains thereto, even though some denizens of the 'higher orders' may stoutly deny it!

Bulls fighting are all part of life's obsession with procreation; and very impressive too!

Bull Fight

We had stooped and splashed an hour or so
Damming this babbling stream
With stone on stone and
Sand handed into crevices.
Father and son, absorbed,
Oblivious in this ancient engineering,
Eager to spill the slipping water to our will
And tell the hills where to fold.

Then we stood; rather he did,
While I ached upright by degrees
Blinking at the bright cattle meadow
Yellow and blue brushed with wild flowers,
Miraged by the wind shimmer and the warmth.
But there was more than shimmer.
There was dust and a torus of whirling cattle,
Bull centred and satellited by moons
Of hectic heifers and craven calves,
Silent, but running circles,
Caught by the gravity of the fight.

From our furlong we scanned the drama,
Rooted and wondrous, ankles awash.
Our mind's eye quick pitched forward
To pencil in details from the Front,
Propagandered by our expectations.

Above the stir and herd backs stood
Two barrel bodied bulls
Humped and horn locked low for leverage
Head to head they eyed each other
With vein bulging black defiance.

It seemed the quarters did the work.
Both stood, fore feet firm,
Leaning, waiting, galloning breath,
While behind each blade and small advantage,
Each tussock felt and found was used
With a thrust that arched and
Lighteninged up the spine,

Pivoting sinuous at the shoulder,
Half hoisting the opponent with its force.

And the effort!
What Newtons
And hoof pounds of wasted work
As the bulls drove back and forth.
But was it wasted? Who knows.
We were not privy to their purpose.

Then from the milling moon run
Two splay eyed calves sped,
Straight for us like fragments,
Lowing urgent as they fled,
Uncertain whether to or from.
They calved in half the furlong
Before our silhouettes slowed their escape
And arched them slowly round,
Accelerating to the pulling passions
Of the elders of their kind.

Suddenly, by agreement, it was over:
And others, romping now in safe excitement
Took up the theme for sport and show,
With more relief than resolution.
Only the winner was still mooned around
With moon eyed mates new won to wed.
And one bold beauty,
As if to underscore his victory
And bear upon him responsibilities
His hard won rights conferred,
Mocking mounted him from behind
While the circle of sober sisters
Expected each her own occasion,
Imaged now in this petty indignity.

We could see, as he weary walked away,
The morning's meaning was yet misread
And this tiny triviality but parodied
The lightning to be un-loosed
When the quaking quarters were re- charged.
Then the Newtons' purpose would be plain.

North Bovey 05 06 82

Set Patterns?

Training, be it of dogs, children, soldiers, mathematicians or just fruit trees espaliered against a wall, is a matter of firmly instilling something so that it is then 'set' for life.

The great advantage (and disadvantage) of such set patterns is that, as with espaliers, they become integral, part of us, automatic. That's great if they are for the best, but disastrous if they are not!

Nor is training the only thing that can set patterns in us for life. Trauma achieves it quite well. So can circumstances. Fortunately we are not quite as wooden as espaliers and we can make adjustments for the future.

This is good to know since no one has had ideal circumstances. Everyone has been moulded to some degree. Is our outlook formed by weight of circumstances? Has fear marred or warped our life? Do we react rather than respond, as if something had set a reflex in us? Quite possibly. What we have to question is: which are the set patterns that help? and which are the ones that we sense do not!

With insight and honesty we can recognise them. With determination, and sometimes with help, we can confront them. With courage we can change them, and be quite different thereafter.

But the only person who can change your mind, your attitudes or your set patterns of behaviour, is you - once you see that doing things another way is fundamentally better! Such recognition is the key.

Avocado Stone

The halves of the parental seed
Like lazy lovers caught,
Lay frozen, nested, interbound
Intent upon some silent sound
To energise their deed.

The note was struck; the life force stirred,
And so, with tiny might
The loving seed sent out a root
To claim the soil and feed the shoot,
Before aught else occurred.

Yet stands beneath this seed no soil,
Just water in a jar,
But eager, as the root let down,
And long before a leafy crown,
I watched its daily toil.

Then, as in protest at my stare,
The stone slipped from my hand,
And broke upon the floor, apart
And rolled to rest, with severed heart;
For sundered were the pair.

Yet even so, up grew a shoot,
With scrawny fount of leaves.
It suckled only on the stone,
The half of which had wholly gone,
That bore the pallid root.

And would another grow, in soil,
To give the stem a chance?
For proper ground makes damage good,
As normal nurture surely should
To save what fate would spoil.

And have we, when of slender girth,
Had damage to our soul?
Thank God! We may redress that past!
Not linger, lacking to the last,
Instead, through insight, be re-cast
To gain a true self-worth.

Staines 23 08 91

Incompatible

As so much is blamed on it, what makes for incompatibility? Life and growth go together. Things either grow or die, the steady state is very short! Physical growth reaches a natural size, then stops, but with the right nutrients both personality and character keep evolving.

Just as plants are different and differ in their needs, so do we. Too little (or too much) of a needed nutrient will inhibit, stunt or stop growth, then death begins. The steady state is very short!

Our personal assets of insight, tolerance, care and so forth are what we bring to a relationship. These are the nutrients we offer each other. 'Offer' is deliberately used since insisting is just another form of demand, which halts growth.

If the balance of assets nourishes both parties and permits their personalities and characters to develop and flourish, then there will be compatability even though each may be a very different person with very different backgrounds, interests and ways of looking at life.

Indeed, contrary to the usual idea that compatability is achieved by having similar this and similar that, great diversity need not indicate incompatibility so much as the potential and raw material for a 'growing' relationship.

It is the scope people experience in a relationship for developing personality and character that determines compatability.

How Slender

How slender stands the Poem
By Prose's brawny side,
He, the week-day's workman
She, his prescient bride.

So take they each the other,
Not Death can he they part,
For paired they sing forever
To touch Man's hopeful heart.

Though gross and dull Man's nature,
Without too much disguise,
You two do nurture wisdom;
Through you can Man be wise.

So sing sweet Poem
And say strong Prose,
Record Man's groping quest
And hold it fast so all may see
Our best. Our meagre best.

M40 22 12 91

Power, or Authority?

With very few exceptions, I like children. I like their candour, and if I respond with equal openness and kindness the clean, simple and sturdy relationship deepens.

But a time comes, around about 11, when youngsters become more self conscious; their answers begin to be guarded or tailored to the needs of the circumstances. They have discovered something about discretion, that knowledge is power, and that truth can be painful. But where their trust remains the clean relationship continues.

A paradox faces parents, particularly first timers, but they seldom see it early. Clearly parents do have power in the home, they are the law! But do they have authority? Do they exercise power with the consent of the children, or is there a full blown, full time Resistance Movement well dug in from high chair to high school?

Even very young children understand far more than they have the words to express. If we baby-talk them or deny them our caring candour or pussyfoot with the truth they are confused. But give them openness, truth, fair firmness and insightful explanations geared to their stage, and they recognise and trust the integrity of your word. They see that you understand, and operate in their favour. They are ready to comply, to develop curiosity and self discipline, and to give you the authority to exercise your power in their interests.

It is a subtle business, but it results in free, imaginative and co-operative individuals capable of contributing much to society, not disciplined doormats.

Bond

"Look Daddy, there's trout!"
And she shot her arm out
Along her glance,
Not quite pointing at them.

The slim shadows stood and swerved,
Pushing nowhere in the eddies,
Wheeled suddenly, and were gone.

"Oh! They were there,
I saw them swimming!"
Sad; hung with her intimate elation
She searches for my assurance.

"Yes." I say "I saw them too."
And the splash dappling sun
Is dulled by her smile.
The warmth is deep and secret.

North Bovey 02 06 82

Stability

Historically, making and mixing explosives was a tedious and often somniferous business quite likely to repatriate you prematurely to Kingdom Come!

To avoid this (and the attendant and unwelcome costs and disruption to the employer), employees were given stools with one leg. Nodding off thus became far too unstable and jerky for comfort, and things progressed mostly without a bang.

Where stools, or people, are concerned, stability means three legs. If any leg is weak, weight must be carried carefully, off-centre. But life's burdens land on us indiscriminately and always stress our weakest leg. We try to re-balance by tilting everything towards our firmer props.

Balance in life requires the strong tripod of body, mind and spirit, yet we tend to lavish effort on the first two from lotions to lipo-suction, from play school to PhDs, and overlook the spirit. But when spirit is left un-valued and poorly developed people tend to topple over unexpectedly when heavily burdened. Life becomes unstable and jerky and things go mostly without a bang.

Many things feed the spirit and enable it to thrive and grow, among them music, poetry, or sudden beauty not just seen, but felt.

Beautiful Apples

Beautiful apples nourish.
As much by being
As by eating,
If you let them.

'Algonquin', Deniliquin NSW 08 05 87

In a Barbican Foyer

We had gone to see 'the Scottish play' at the Barbican in London, and while milling with the crowds in the spacious foyers we came across a Geisha dancing to the music of a two- or three-man orchestra of oriental strings.

Her audience was about seventy strong, seated on the floor or the few chairs, standing, or just watching as they passed by.

One man sat on the floor, apart, lotus fashion, absolutely intent and still, wrapped conical in a black cape. He seemed to be part of the performance, a pivot, a fulcrum. He caught my attention.

Contrasts

He sat, black,
Within the throng
Of vacant gazers,
As if floating,
Upon the shoreless floor.
A black lotus bud,
Still as a coal Buddha,

Basalt black he sat,
Black caped, sloping limbs,
Capped by an Astrakhan cloud,
Above his pallid snowline face.
A studied Fujiama,
Brim with subducted senses
And at eruption point,
Roused by the slow and measured flow
Of the Geisha's gradual dances.

Her minute steps
And careful stances
Slip and flow together,
Resilient, brush written,
Subtle as calligraphy
To a learned lover's eye.
Each yielding line, conformed
To the pressure of the art,
Sets forth fresh words,
To sing in formal silence
To the flute and plucking strings
Of the mystic music.

With each new pose
Her clothes enfold
A fresh calligraphy,
Set in gorgeous gold
And green brocades,
Rich, stiff cascades,
With spotless, warm

And pithy white within,
Cuddling his secret inner thoughts.
While with each fresh step
Her slight white cloven foot
Slips to brush aside
Her gown's draped edge
And hint, all white,
(All warm and pithy white)
At secrets coyly hid
Beyond her doll-face mask,
Inviting with her inclined head
But giving nothing more away,
Except with fingertips
Where everything she says is said.

Staines 11 04 87

A Day Away

Bluff Hilll in Napier, New Zealand, stands quite alone, rising abruptly from the flat, like next door's Ayers Rock. It is however vigorously treed, somewhat valleyed and fully developed as the 'best part of town'. It also forms a fair promontory into the South Pacific. These minor incongruities aside, the two do have a certain impact-similarity from a distance!

My father bought a gracious home on Bluff Hill, with wide views and wide verandahs. It looked north through a Jacaranda tree, across a stepped lawn springy to the point of instability, past an elegant gum, and over Hawke's Bay and the yachts to the far off hills on the other shore.

Around Staines, in Middlesex, England, where I live, there are no dramatic landscape features unless you count Heathrow which, in time honoured airport tradition, is rather unbluff. It is however very busy, very big, and not as noisy as it might be!

Not so long ago the Roman town of Staines was a day's journey from London, with several picturesque inns to put up in and stabling for horses. Now, with Heathrow right next door, Staines is only a day's journey from almost any spot on earth, and inns (the 'Inncontinental', the 'Travelator', the 'Throttlodge' and the "Terminal Apron') have Porche parking.

From London to Staines by horse, or Porche, lets one integrate time and distance – body and mind arrive united. But twenty to thirty hours of circumglobal jetting moves matter faster than mind, particularly post-forty mind. For days the disintegrated remains of your otherwise orderly head come staggering in like lost luggage. In the meantime one tends to feel a little dis-orient-autralasia'd!

Jet Lag

As I move about the world
I part both space and time
I am at once both
Here! & Now!
And am at once at Home.
The inner and the outer me
Exist and overlap,
Both hand in hand
And worlds apart,
I am the two in one.

Napier, NZ 15 05 87

Ringside

Waikato River runs deep, crystal clear and quiet out of Lake Taupo in the middle of the North Island, New Zealand, and within a mile or two is confronted by a smooth-topped band of rock that seems to up-well across its path forming a step, from the land upstream into the wide bowl below.

There may have been a time when Waikato simply flooded against this wall and over ran it smoothing the top and digging the bowl as it crashed beyond, but water, or possibly seismic activity, has cracked a cleft in this band of rock through which Waikato runs today, with impressive results!

The cleft, a straight though not a clean break, maybe 250 yards long and 30 feet wide, drops the river perhaps 30 feet before it reaches the fall. Upstream, the river seems to stand just a foot or so below the rock edge and from a little distance you could easily miss this little gorge. The tourist path comes square at it and takes you straight over on a small foot bridge, two yards above the cold, bright, blue and white demented water seething with quite extraordinary force!

At the far end of the cleft the fall is magnificent not for any great height, but for the great speed and the concentrated volume of water leaping out of the rock into the vast and boiling pool below. This is…

Huka Fall

Emerald green and greener,
Deep, undercliff and full
Waikato flows from Taupo
Toward the Huka Fall.

Deep muscles well up ripples,
Dark waters, crystal roll,
Ready for the battle
Joined at Huka Fall.

Glassy smooth, advancing,
Then dancing to the call,
Comes the great Waikato
To fight at Huka Fall.

Then through the gorge he thunders
And tears the rocky wall,
Surging through the battle
That's fought at Huka Fall.

Then, at the end Waikato
Leaps down the gorge end wall
And spews himself almighty
Beyond the Huka Fall.

Still seething from the action
He boils mid misty pall,
Then calm to glassy smoothness
Departs from Huka Fall.

Napier, NZ 25 05 87

Out of the Foyer into the Frying Pan!

With a day to myself in Melbourne I spent it mostly in the Art Gallery, looking, thinking, feeling, and trying to soak in something of what others had said about Australia and being Australian from ancient time to the present.

For a while, rather like another statue, I sat quietly on one of the broad upholstered square benches in a corner room connecting two long galleries, looking at the exhibits.

A school party was bore-ing through the gallery that day, all about 12. Eventually they shoaled past me in a curricular quest for culture, vacant gazing, biros and mangled project sheets in hand.

The armature of this poem was written there, on the third or fourth floor, but it was finished off in a foyer of the Royal Children's Hospital a couple of miles away an hour or two later, as I waited to meet my wife and sister-in-law.

Since I was waiting in the wrong foyer, there was plenty of time to finish the poem, but I didn't win any Brownie points!

An Oz accent does enhance the flavour!

Beholders

Boys tumble and toss
Jostling eagerly past
Busts and statuary;
These bold bronze casts,
Worked with master's craft
To show slow followers the way.

"That's Art ...!" they shout,
"y' know - Real Art!"
And snigger off
Scurrying from bum to bum,
Quips wicked on their tongue,
To point, and hoot, and run,
Raspberrying their own
Graven ancestors.

Now gymslip girls gather round
And flush ambitious,
Envying the brazen breasts,
The thighs, the eyes
That stare you out,
Unpricking; unashamed;
And yearn to be so -
Unabashed!

"Oh Please! I want to be
A brazen lady too!"
They sigh within,
As eager under modest lids
The maiden eyes soak in
The sheer potential of the bronze
And show it in their skin!

They tear themselves away
Unable to bear the wait
These promised insights bring
They tear themselves away
To wait their powerful day ... ,

While the smutty boys cheer on,
Snorting vulgar, two galleries away,
Blithely unaware
Of all, that one day,
Will be required of them.

Melbourne Art Gallery 06 05 87

'The Troubles'

When 'the Troubles' in Northern Ireland started again, the news held my attention a while until the tangled issues confused me; then irritation took over. After all, they were far off, and nothing to do with me. (It shocked me to discover that I lived closer to 'The Troubles' than to Glasgow!). Gradually my indifference became uneasy. Ignoring human tragedy just next door in the hope that it would go away was inadequate. My Belfast-born wife felt the same way. We began asking, listening, trying to grapple with the mysteries and fit together something of the background. It was not easy. For their own 'hot house' reasons, propagandists on both sides had achieved shut-out. Truth, did of course emerge, but usually far from the whole truth.

Eventually, to the overt concern of many friends, we decided to holiday in Northern Ireland with our children. We went to tour the whole province with open hearts and a willingness to listen, to ask anyone and everyone for their perceptions, insights, hopes, fears and dreams and to think and feel into the situation as much as we could.

We read broad-based Irish history before we went, without that, many conversations would simply have seemed cryptic, so much of the matter is so old. Over 800 years many real wrongs have been done by those from both sides of the Irish Sea.

That first visit, brief, and superficial as it was, completely re-furnished my mind on Ireland and made me look hard at myself. My pride in being British had been self satisfied and blind. I had not even imagined there might be a less edifying side; I had not walked one step in another man's shoes to see if they hurt him!

I began to see that people who feel wronged, historically, by a nation I represent with pride, may easily see my silence about their old wounds not as ignorance, but as tacit endorsement of the past. So why trust me any more than my perpetrating forbears!

To win their trust I must first care, then acknowledge and apologise for the ancient wrongs of my nation. I must accept the old guilts as my own! Why? Because they still hurt the people I would be friends with. Not a comfortable insight, but illuminating!

'The Troubles' have old historical roots set in sour soil. Before any verdant new growth can occur those old roots must be set into fresh and fertile soil. Patriotic inheritors, on both sides, must put a fresh, honest tilth in place of their forefather's sour soil; naming, acknowledging and fairly apologising for each old wrong, in their forefather's stead.

Only those aggrieved can forgive but when people see real remorse for wrongs done, full forgiveness is seldom far behind. Reconciliation occurs between those who say sorry, and those with big hearts who accept that apology and forgive, be the parties individuals or nations. People may then restore each other to honour and trust, with a rich new tilth to root in.

If relatively few individuals were to cross the Irish Sea to open their hearts, meet and go deep enough with care and concern to build bridges the 'Irish Problem' would begin to resolve. Bridges to carry friendship and concern each way are needed. Simply trying to blow froth off the political Guinness from a safe distance will not work!

This poem was written during our first visit. I am encouraged that parts of the poem were quoted in a Northern Ireland debate in the House of Lords and may be seen in Hansard.

Not the Bitter Men

When he spoke
His syllables were scented,
Laden with mist
And the ring of forefathers,
But our crude ears
Were not cued to his cadence
And we stumbled among his sounds.
Off balanced.

For a while there was distance between us.
Our antiseptic English
Gave us away to him,
Prying friendliness apart
Under the weighty wedge of history.
Just from our voices
There was latent fear released.
This common language
At first allowed
Only the accentuation
Of our differences,
Leaving but our hearts to pound,
And ponder leaping such a gulf.

But heart and heart respond
When interest in the other shows,
And gradually the jagged edge
Of buried fear is overgrown,
Mossed softer through care
And the green seedling Trust;
On this ancient mound.

"Since flint was knapped
Chiefs and Queens
Older than the Irish
Have held this drumlin
Against all odds.
Here were heroes
And legends made.

Here have been sung
Songs older than Christ
By a thousand years ...
But all things pass ... "

These skeins he laid out lovingly,
Proud of his ancient past
Quenching questions,
Arcing up to his vantage point,
Safe on this mound,
This early ground
Before Baginbun.

Then, as the story ran
So it filled, flowing with blood,
Injustice and defeat;
The whiff of smoke,
As bitterness burned
Deep in the Irish peat.
But peat is slow consumed
And even in old ashes
Old fears feed the embers
Until yawning prejudice
Dries young
Trust to tinder
Yet again,
And Ireland burns!

Man cannot live by bread alone.
That only permits existence.
But fear is the milk
Suckling the generations here.
Subtle as Sunday and Home.
Flying in the air like fall-out.
Man cannot live
By fear alone.
But fear is here,
Stalking in the mown grass
High on this hillock,
Empty but for us
And the small boy

Tugging up his kite in the breeze.
But the fear our new friend felt
Was not of us, the strangers;
He feared his own,
Like one who had let down the drawbridge
Of his own beleaguered town
But could not run away!
His frankness had shocked him
And he stood up of a sudden
To see where his words were blown,
That he might gather them back again
To stop the wind
Incriminating him.

So youth stands bound!
Strapped by the filaments
Of name and place.
Caught by the brazen Christs
Set up by bitter men
To rally fears around.

Father forgive them
For they know not
... How can they?
How can they see
Your Son from beneath
The glaciation of history
Full of overburden and debris
Belonging nowhere;
Trapped by the sheer pressures
Of the implacable ice?

But even as this landscape shows,
There is a warmth
That melts such ice.
A Holy microwave,
Exciting at each core
That precious drop of free moisture
We call our Humanity.
God forbid that that should freeze
For that is just what Evil is after

No one has the answer.
We are all too enmeshed.
There is no nostrum,
No political proposition
To make fear illegal.
Only Trust does that
When heart and heart respond,
Then risk rebuff and pain
To hold the other's hurts
And recognise one's blame;
Asking - for deep forgiveness.

Yet Trust and Faith are brothers
Lost in a land steeped in Christianity!
Is it that Ireland
Now only believes in God
Without trusting Him?
That is what fear has done!
That's the havoc it can wreak!
By being deaf we make Him dumb
Forbidding Him to speak! Denying
God the daily chance
To show each one their part
In His gentle master plan.

If that is all, there is hope indeed!
Faith is but a step beyond belief
For any willing to be obedient.
And God knows,
The Irish have been obedient.
The metal of these men is good!
Europe stands firm,
Founded on the love and learning
Of those early, fearless Irish,
When they first let God lead.

This Celtic culture
Then gave the world so much,
And will do so again
When God is once more in the lead,
And not the bitter men!

Owen, a Catholic, is the person in the first line. The day after we met him
Sheila and I both felt compelled to return to the monument where he was
working to invite him to come for an evening meal to our holiday cottage
near Cookstown.

It was perhaps rash and risky, (certainly our friends would have said so!)
but unless one steps forward, one stays rooted. Owen came. Quite a
courageous decision on his part.

Over the intervening years the friendship has grown. Owen has been to
our home on numerous occasions and we to his. In 1991 he married a
Protestant bride in Belfast and we went to the wedding. One close friend
wanted to meet me to discuss this poem. It had seemingly been a pivot
in Owen's life and in his thinking about The Troubles and could he, the
friend, have a copy.

A 'bridge' has been established and is being strengthened every time we meet
or talk on the phone. Much that is valuable may yet pass over it.

Evening in the Burren

We were driving a high road in the Burren enjoying the sun slipping to the horizon, when we noticed the dolmen, down sun to our left, a couple of hundred yards away.

It was quite hard to see the old stones camouflaged against the rocky background, so we stopped and walked over to look at them.

The land here only thinly clothes its limestone bones like a pauper's worn rags. We moved with caution, eyes down, avoiding the many cracks and rocky ankle traps. So we seemed to arrive at the ancient megaliths abruptly.

The impact was thus more powerful. The hey presto! arrival, the remote openness, the the sense of having been transported there, was strong. The legacy of old lore lay thick on the place, protective, then gradually it drew aside and we marvelled at our inclusion.

Dolmen

You might miss it,
If your eye was only open
Into your mind,
You might not see,
But pass on by
Gazing at the scene unseen,
Like a tourist.

But if your eye was open,
If the lens was clear,
You would see not just grey stones,
But the Dolmen,
Set up here when Man's span
Was just a little ledge,
Jutting from the monolith of time.

But see now!
Wash away today,
And catch the ebb of time
Between you and these stones.
Touch them, and compress
Four thousand years
Between your finger tips
And the stone!
Then look again.
See what you have made!
Here, in this limestone land,
Where the gryked ground
Gulps rain away
With a cavernous thirst.
Look at the Dolmen.
Think what you have done!

It will not be missed!
The moon will fill and
Children's children come,
Beyond the counting
Of your hands on this stone;

Many, and many more!
And all will see
That you were here
Sweating these stone slabs
Into the future,
Erect, trebated crude and clever;
Quite beyond the hope
Or Faith of future man
For his own posterity.

But mind most well
The mystery of your skill
For therein lies your Dolmen's power!
Let that slip and it becomes
Grey old stones, but un-enchanted!
So mind your spell.
Draw them, year by year
To wonder, touch and stare.

Now, as you lift your hand,
Time tide floods full in,
Filling four thousand years
Brim with things to move man
From these old stones
To the very stars.

And yet, Ancient One,
Your Dolmen is a challenge!
Your compass was these hills
Yet your horizon was Eternity.
While we, careless of tomorrow,
Sift the radio mist of Creation
For signs of what was once,
To find from whence we come.
How could you see so far?
What was your certainty?

And yet we sense it
For we come, and come
To snap off exact moments

With short buzz saw shutters
Then eager, pointing at the image
Declare "Look what man did
All that time ago",
Keen to claim our roots
In your achievements,
By brief propinquity!

But even this is not enough.
Beyond your Dolmen, ours;
In quick and tiny profusion,
As close as they dare creep,
To gain prestige by association.

Mere mocking models these,
Crude fashioned, mean,
Reflecting their makers,
As does your Dolmen you.
Yours, a resting place for time
While ours form a necropolis,
To harbour our un-voiced need
To look toward Eternity.

You were and are ahead of us
For we only begin to dimly see
What it is your Dolmen has to say.

Staines 09 09 89

Sugar and Salt

Despite these 'common law' times, marriage is booming, but with society's lack of vision for marriage, how to stay married is a real problem!

Unfulfilled immature expectations on either side, or self-centred attitudes, bring disillusion and finger pointing with all its implied demand. And demand doesn't work! Point the finger instead at what you can put right, 'adjusting' involves him, or her, and you!

A good marriage suits both partners and enables each to develop, mature and tackle 'mountains'with an ally. Where partners jointly have vision about what their marriage is for, they set a course, hoist sails, and have a rudder by which to steer!

It takes great courage to be truly honest but all relationships thrive when mutual honesty lets the other see strengths, vulnerability, and pleas for forgiveness, as they really are. From honesty grow trust and respect, both of which are damaged each time one is forced to fumble through a fog of fabrication for the whole truth.

'All out love', the carefree, unguarded, marriage type, grows directly from trust and respect. And it must be freely given first, and equally freely accepted. Engagement is a time for deep honesty and discovery!

For abundant growth, keep love's roots – honesty and trust – moist, give love plenty of light and fresh air, deal immediately with any problems. Never put love in a hothouse and don't be afraid to use a delicate pinch of salt occasionally, to cleanse it and keep it fresh.

Friends

I have a friend, he's called Honesty.
He and I met many moons ago.
I didn't like him; pricking conscience!
I tried to kill him as a deadly foe.

I fought against him. He fought for me!
Honesty kept winning, round by round.
Then I caught his eye, smiling, carefree,
Saw there integrity and changed my ground.

I have a friend, (so has Honesty.)
Our friend is Trust, and he's good fun!
Trust is a linguist, open, approachable,
Speaks every language under the sun!

Trust is risky, bold and adventurous.
Open hearted and a faithful friend.
Never niggardly, always simple,
Knows human nature, but does not pretend!

I have a friend who joined us recently.
He is strong, yet supple as a glove.
Honesty knew him; told me about him.
Trust introduced me to my new friend, Love.

He is a mystery, deeply thoughtful,
Always ahead of one's every need!
Love is gentle, visionary, passionate,
Whether one is strong or a broken reed.

Honesty and Trust, these are sturdy friends.
They join me daily, as I work with Love.
But if I stray away Honesty comes after me,
Then hard behind him come Trust and Love!

Staines 08 09 89
For Ross on his Fifteenth Birthday with Love

Ross, aged 15.

In through the Cat Flap!

Some poems fall onto paper and need only minimum adjustment. This was one of them.

I was sitting working at my desk in the window on a warm September day when this poem arrived unannounced, commandeered my pen and scrawled itself over my scrap pad.

Somewhat surprised I gathered it up, pushed it about a bit with the biro, then filed it with the others and got back to what I was doing.

But my concentration was perforated all day by surprise and covert excitement. I don't feel I wrote it, it was given.

Timeless Mind

The timeless mind in all of us
Distils old wisdom slow,
To help prevent the fall of us
By giving us to know
Of seasoned thought
From aeons past;
And new thought fit to sow.
The timeless mind in all of us
Permits the soul to grow.

The choice is ours, for all of us,
To wither or to climb;
To heed the ancient call in us,
Or grovel in our grime
Where fear ejects
All wisdom's faith
And frosts the heart with rime,
'Till timeless mind in all of us
Becomes but mindless time.

Staines 21 09 82.

Arrested Development

The older I grow the more I discover a case of arrested development! Now, in certain ways that can be enviable, but every so often I react incongruously, not true to what I would expect from me, and I stop to look into what makes me behave as I do, to explain, not excuse myself.

Lurking in my past I find an often lonely lad who, due to circumstances, was in various boarding schools from an early age. Without a day-to-day involved adult to help me make head or tail of things I did the best I could. My conclusions satisfied facts as I saw them and were not only immature but frequently unsound, yet my simple answers became immured in the walls that made the developing me, and there they are today, holding me up! But I notice that some of the bricks there are not even of my making or laying. Some were merely mortared in by hurtful events, without any selection of mine.

Early in our marrriage I used to get angry and irrationally upset when talking to my wife if she was knitting. That traced back to my early teens when another loved one sprang devastating news on me, knitting attentively throughout. How callous that was! How it salted my anguish! How it smouldered! How it warped that relationship for years, until I saw beyond my pain to hers. She had knitted to retain hold of her own emotions, but I had assumed otherwise.

Insight enabled me to apologise for the bitter consequences of my misreading of that event. That relationship has been restored and knitting no longer riles me. Not a bad haul for a little digging and some specific apology. So step by step, at what always seems a high price, I am replacing dodgy old brickwork. It does however seem worth it as the real me is emerging stronger, albeit slowly and somewhat late.

I notice though that I'm not unique. There seem to be quite a few rather old teenagers about. Perhaps they are quietly replacing dodgy brickwork too!

Growing Pain

Strewboulder paths,
In child-hood climbs,
Or up youth's eager scree,
Can bruise bring any climber
To bloodied hand and knee.

As more and more it hurts us
We tend our aching needs
Delaying our development,
To shield a heart that bleeds.

Slowly we accustom
To the damage of our past.
We smile, we strike a posture,
And strive from first to last
To paper up the hollow hell
In which our lonely spirits dwell,
Pretending that within our shell,
A lion heart beats fast.

But, see the scars of infancy,
Then touch them with your heart
And heal them, for we have the power
To make a true accountancy.

For what we do stays worthless
And life goes on, misplaced
Draped with awful debris
Until past hurts are faced;
o Lord, forgive the lies we live,
And to our help make haste.

Then grasp our eager out-stretched arm
And on our life impart,
The mark of your involvement;
An eager out-stretched heart.

Tirley 02 09 91

Designing

I can roll my tongue unto a tube and stick it out. Not a show stopper I know, but my wife cannot, nor can she wink her left eye. She is just not wired up that way. From technical drawings I can create solid reality in my mind, others cannot. Surely if they just tried a bit..? But I guess it's all down to basic wiring!

Design is prophetic and needs another sort of circuit too, one set to conjure with the future. The designer's inner eye needs video vividness to see, move round, and inspect that which does not exist. This other world is only accessible to others through the language of drawn form, line, volume, colour and texture. Few speak it well, far more read it, but sadly some don't even know the language exists!

Thinking in Hungarian may not transport one to Hungary, but design transports designers, just ask my wife. Environment, time, and place, all become fluid when one sets about predicting the detailed evolution of what is to be. Future possible, present actual and past fact may be walked into, commandeered, changed, moved, juxtaposed or evaluated. Anything needed can be considered. Anything can be adjusted to suit at any moment. The decision is yours. It is a heady, powerful realm, this other world!

So it should be no great surprise that some cannot follow easily. Yet it becomes hard to explain again and again, one aches to take those bound by here and now, those who see only today or at best next week, to see this future place, to experience its potential.

I wonder what antiquaries feel? I guess that future-hungry designers must seem rather brash when there is so much already here to find out about.

Future Shores

My shiny spindled key
Jabs chatty at the office lock,
Which, waking dry
From stare-eyed night security,
Turns dead in its mortise,
Drawing the bolt for the day
That I may be imprisoned,
Concentrated in this cell;
Equipped - complete with sandwiches.

Here whole leagues of life have passed,
Hosed along, all important,
Running on the scud and flush of ideas:
Those rippling tsunamis rolling
To break with what force -
On what shore?
You might ask.

Must this crest and score of experience
Rush steep with solutions
Through the shallows and petty pools,
Breaking to foam and scatter
In splashy gouts of spout and spray
Against the all coralling reefs
Of tide checking bureaucracies?

Is it ever to run strong
Up the hot sun strand,
To sweep the flotsam sand-fringe free
And show the sharp simplicity
Of order from prevailing chaos?
Is such a notioned ocean tide
Always to be reefed back,
Or does the flotsam merely have to float,
Once the ringing reef is drowned
By the level - rather than the force?
You might ask.

Here my heart hopes have flown
Blowing and soaring, lines on lines,
Architecture tumbling into form,
From skein to scene,
Concreted by the intimacy that is designing,

So that I at least have been and seen:
Have trod the tide swept fringes of the mind
Knowing the reality that could be,
Unable to invite others there
Save the occasional other dream seer
Able to walk with thoughts and see.

But to live, to really be alive,
This future state must co-exist
With now and be subtled through
The mesh and official sieve,
(Which fillets the future possible
Of guts and bones
As if they were out of plaice)
So that enough of thought and form
Survives to fresh pebble
Some small far stretch of the tide line.
So by degrees the level rises
Above the point where little polyps sting,
And the mind tide floods me free again
To walk the future shores.

Then, with day-end energy done
The mind winds back to now,
Though splashing still
Up far off thought streams:
More now in snapshot than in fact.

And mundane I jingle my jacket
For the key to secure the future overnight
While the lock waits
Keen eyed and bolt bated,
Ready to shoot the tiny gap
Between these inner and outer worlds.

Then I am freed; empty as my lunch-box,
To be re-charged by home life,
Simple sanity,
And the zest and promise of children.

Staines 11 07 82

Poetry

Creativity is an odd business. When I design a building or a product I need to steep myself for a week or more in the detailed requirements until they form part of me. Then, seemingly without conscious thought, key ideas pop up from which the design flows. The subconscious has been working on it! It happens with writing too.

Having been asked to write a piece on talents I set to, conviction in one hand, concentration in the other, and started onto paper, but I could not capture the flavour I sought. Instead, out flopped porridge not prose! I recognised the symptoms so I did something else instead!

A few days later, in the quiet of a cottage near Dartmoor, the subconscious having rolled the oats awhile, turned porridge into poem, and it flowed.

But what is poetry? Some poems have parade ground precision, some rhyme or scan, others move with a sort of free Brownian motion, other run as water drops down a thread. And when is one a poet? Is one's Poetic Licence given by general consensus or after some objective test so that Poetic Justice is seen to be done?

For me, poetry is writing that is sparser but resonates more than prose. It creates nuances that make the reader participate to complete the poetic process. In so doing the audience may perceive more in the poem than the poet. Great!

Nor is poetry exclusive. Most people can be lifted or amused, expanded or touched by the ancient power of meter, or the ring and chime of rolling rhyme. Poems need not be great to be worth reading, but they should reach into and illuminate something within the reader. Nor is poetry some arcane art, but quite a common, if not so often realised, talent of many.

Talents

His hands move,
Mighty with Grace and Love.
Gently He moulds immortal form
Endowing each new soul
In this moment of creation ...
With Angels!

Again He moves,
To put each soul
Among the molecules
And spiral super-spaces
Of mortal man,
Where each Angel,
His gift of skill and powers,
Binds herself, obedient,
No longer to the Maker's will,
But as He wills, - to ours!

Then as we go our wilful ways
We gradually spurn
The Godly call of Graces given
And gradually learn
A Pride for each new skill.
We shame each Angel turn by turn
And then each Angel kill!
Oh Lord! Oh Angels! Forgive lost hours
Of sweat and chafe for other's powers,
Sent for other souls!
You gifted talents,
Angels with our name,
Express through us our Maker's will
And sing of whence you came!
Our hands He moves
And with them He reveals
Enough of brightness,
Angel given,
As is good for us to see of Heaven.

North Bovey 26 12 83

They Know Not What They Do

I've known men work for 'the family' so hard they seldom see their family, don't nurture family life, and feel bitter, bewildered and betrayed when they end up without it.

We all need to feel worthwhile, appreciated by others, but a sense of low worth, if we were not encouraged and valued as a child, can lead the adult to strive compulsively for visible affirming success.

Providing well for one's family makes public your worthy effort, responsible attitude, success and respect-ability. But it also justifies more striving, while the family yearns for a loved one's presence, interest, involvement and time! A subtle loop.

Blood relationship does not make a family, caring relationships do. Open your heart and anyone can become part of your family, close it and no one can! If work comes before the family they soon recognise their secondary worth. How can they feel worthwhile and valued if those they long to love give them scant personal attention or time?

Parents build inadequacies into children with frightening ease! In our early years we learn how to relate, how (or if) to love. Return a child's outgoing warmth with fun, attention and cuddles and the technique is repeated, loving is learned. Ignore them, make ineffective their out-going warmth, and it will be replaced by approval seeking, demanding, confrontation, and manipulation for advantage.

Such unattractive behaviour strains relationships and attenuates caring. The loop is reinforced, the child grows up feeling unloved, bitter and inadequate. They may then sink or fight. Fighters simply decide which side of the law suits them best, but fighting is seldom constructive or attractive! "Man! Where are you going?"

Quo Vadis

"Man!
Where are you going?"
Your body has no answer.
It's interests are immediate,
And given them, is sullen silent.
But you discomfort it, even slightly,
Then hear it's selfish scream!
It has no other answer, or concern.

"Where are you going?"

From where you stand,
The mind, proud knowing mind,
Will mull the matter at a safe remove,
Not to be drawn in too deep,
And flattered, will gravely spin
A web of steps and strategies
To answer subtly, or so it seems,
Basing all on hopes and health and opportunity.
Predicting what it is powerless to effect.

"Where are you going?"

A deeper note begins to ring
When you ask your Spirit.
Now, unless you know,
It bangs and clangs about
Until you slam the lid of thought
Upon it, to stifle light and air,
Hoping it will die,
Or seep away.

"Where are you going?"

'How can I know!
How can I even begin;
Not knowing who I am or why I'm here!?
For what purpose?'

Man needs a purpose.
Speed alone is not effective,
For efforts, like arrows,
Unleash with a proud twang!
Crisp! Impressive!
At rumoured targets in the fog.
And like the fog the question clings,
Ever insistent in your head,
Severing escape from sleep,
And making it uneasy.
It needs an answer
So that restfulness may return.

"Where are you going Man?"

'Why do you ask me such questions!
They disturb me!'
"But I do not; it is you.
Deep within, your very bones know,
The question is the lock of life,
For which each must find the key."
Find it and the fog falls back.
No longer does it obscure ... ,
Or protect.
Neither now is your fortress needed
For you see each adversary,
Swaddled in his own fog,
Noisy, calling for your position
So that he may aim his shot.
You though are nimble now
Needing only the light armament of life;
Honesty, perception and high hope
With courage to face reality,
Out on this bright plane.

"Man! Where are you going!"

Out on this bright plane ...
Man needs a purpose,
Far off, elemental, outside himself,

That he might work with others.
Existence is not disputed, only
Why?
Just being is not a reason!
Neither is having.
Fulfillment is no purpose,
But a by product of becoming,
Of growth and change,
Of maturity, of wisdom,
Not of knowing or possessing!

"Where are you going?

On the marionetted path of expediency,
Eager into petty death,
Or pacing measured breath for stride
To the eye-wide horizon
Where Kingdom comes on Earth,
As it is in Heaven?"
There is a purpose!
God-wide and given, to us,
His small and tarnished artifacts,
Loved unreasonably,
So that we may share, for simple asking,
The final polishing of His creation!
Thy will be done ... !
How can we be so blind
To miss the clue
And expend our life and effort
On thickening the fog?
But He sees through us to the core
And loves us now, and as we might yet be,
If love can lure us
From our fear of freedom,
Our yearning for recognition
And acceptability ... by whom?

"Where are you going, complex Man?

'Lord! I sense but fear the way!

My courage quails to see the inner me
And risk such exposure!
I am raw, scabbed by scraping time!
Peeled of purpose;
On the edge; Irrelevant!
How can I admit,
Such hopelessness; and hope?
"Come!
Stand safe,
Here in My palm.
Have life and joy contagious!
Be a wise and simple fool for Me ...

Staines 09 05 83

Testing for God

In all truth, I am not a natural believer. I wish I was, instead I need quite a bit of convincing! Until I reached thirty five I was ambivalent about religion. Only when I met a man I saw was 'effective', did Christianity's promises begin to appear realistic. I was challenged, and very warily I looked into the matter.

But if you go looking for God you cannot find what is not there, so first you must at least permit him to exist, and then look for supporting evidence!

The first 'evidence' I could see was my friend. "Experiment. Pray. Listen. Obey." he had said. "Science searches, with diligence, rigour and control, advancing slowly, methodically, and carefully recording observed phenomena. You can look for God this way too, without any outside help."

So I experimented, as he had suggested. The rate of coincidences rose dramatically and with it my interest. Six months later belief became a quiet realisation not a decision, and faith has been a mixture of heady excitement and hapless stumbling towards a greater trust ever since.

And I am helped by the thought that if I did have certainty about things faith would be irrelevant! So my doubts are not in vain; I can go forward holding to what I do know and putting difficult questions in the 'awaiting more light' box.

This poem was written early one Easter morning in Holland, during my quiet time before rising.

Easter

Oh risen Christ
I
gradual
See
The meaning
Of
your Death
For me.
Your hideous pain is mine to bear!
My shame, my sin, you took my share,
And Smelted Out
Upon the
Cross
The gold
For me
And took
The dross
Of sin And bore
It clean Away,
That I Might
Rise
With
Hope
Today!

A poem that
Leaves you at
the foot
of the
cross.

Wassenar 03 04 83

Inner Compass

We are all concerned to achieve our potential, not to miss out, to feel accepted for what we are, in our own and each other's eyes. So we study and strive and are inclined to inflate our abilities a bit and, try as we might, it is hard to act according to our conscience and do what we hold to be right. The temptation is to seek other's recognition or approval, and so fall into 'people pleasing'.

Now pleasing people is a lovely by-product of right conduct but as an objective it becomes a chronic disease. Contrary to intention, it robs the people pleaser of the affirmation and self worth he seeks. It makes him or her into a moral cripple, externally dependent on other's opinions. The people pleaser's constant fear is that they may be unappreciated. And they are!

But our real potential is, by definition, inbuilt, there to be realised, developed and deployed. We have been given everything needed for a stimulating and appreciated life, even down to the compass by which to steer it! Consult that compass, follow the tough course it points and moral courage, inner dependability, and self respect – all embryonic – will develop.

The force that aligns the inner compass is not deflected by culture or background. It is pan-human, deeper than mere cultural choice and points unerringly between wisdom and folly, right and wrong, evolution and degeneration, human and sub-human. It will guide anyone, if they let it. Follow this steady compass and we start to realise our potential and then to realise our potential is more than we would have dared to believe!

Fisherman

Sudden, at noon-day, Youth heard a calling,
Stopped in his gamboling; stock still stood he.
Stood on his island, safe on the dry land;
Stood on the high land and looked at the sea.
Deep in the background, far in his hearing,
Heard he his calling; what he should be.

"I want a fisherman, wily and daring:
I want a fisherman to fish me the sea.
Take you a faithful line, tautened to breaking,
Catch me a great catch; as there should be."
Deep, in the background, just in his hearing
Heard he this calling to fish him the sea.

Stood he on dry land, scanned the horizons,
Thought he his thoughts on the catches to be.
Wove he a line from fine thoughts, persuasions,
Cast he this subtle line into the sea.
Deep, to the black ground, far from his hearing,
Sank he the line he made, into the sea.

Deep in this darkness sank he this subtle line,
Fishing for big fish, deep in the sea,
Patient he sought them, vainly he waited,
Sat on his safe shore, safe from the sea.
Deep, in the background, just in his hearing,
Heard he the Lord say "Listen to me!"

"I want a fisherman, wily and daring:
I want a fisherman who listens to me.
Seek first to know the fish, there, in the ocean~
Next, use My insight, for then you will see
Deep into backgrounds, far beyond hearing
How to catch big fish: then catch them, for Me."

Then stood Youth staring, surveying the ocean,
Feared he the Powers which now he could see:
Saw he into it, and all that it held there.

Said he, 'I'll go there, if Thou go with me.'
Deep, to the black ground, swam he, tuned to Him,
Met he the Sinners that dwell in the sea.

Down he dived deeply, flooded by salt tide,
Down swam he strong to the stretch of his lung.
Drank he there nothing, but saw he there plenty,
Breathed he no breath there, but listened he long
Deep, in the background, yet in his hearing,
Heard he God speaking, quiet, steady and strong!

Back on the dry land, safe on the island,
Washed in pure water to clean off salt sea,
Planned he the fishing, planned he the catching,
Gave he his life, for the fishing to be.
Deep, in the background, heard he God calling
"Fisher; fish Sinners, then love them - for me!"

Staines 29 06 86

Passing

Mystery, all is mystery. Strange, the marble cool of a carcass when the spark has gone. That is the tell tale of passing; life is warmth.

Grief and wonder mix at times of quiet passage. Life steals away, no big deal. Wonder that a moment slim as tissue paper, separates the now from the next. Wonder that something unique crosses, seeps through, never to return.

Grief that leaves such an ache even when the death is timely, assured and expected.

Mystery all.

Where a Loved One Died

Impassive house
How can you stare
Clear paned at such a time,
While Death and Spring
Both mingle
And heartache breaks within?

How do you stand
Unmoved, while I,
At sunshine's touch, do weep?
What strengthens you
While blowing blooms
Engorge my choking throat?

You stand unmoved,
Green gardened round,
While epochs close within
And tidal tears
Deep drown mine eyes
And dim the sun to glim.

So stand mature,
Green gardened round,
Without the life within,
And as that soul
So I'll depart,
Yet feel the parting sting.

Impassive house
How can you stare
Clear paned at such a time,
While Death and Spring
Both mingle
And heartache breaks within?

Napier 16 11 91

Supernatural or Unperceived?

Organisms, us included, seek 'comfy' conditions. But comfort stops development.

"But," you cry "if comfortable, what development do you need?" It's a fair point, but only if comfort is our highest aim.

Comfort may be physical, with one's inner life of thought and ideal; or in another realm, the spiritual.

Now, the supernatural is hard to credit as real, but a mere candle of an idea threw light on it for me.

Consider: The options open to inorganic matter are to combine or accrete. To minerals all else is supernatural. But let life, root or microbe, touch and lay claim to inorganic matter and it is transformed into organic, living, matter. Yet thought and reason are still clearly supernatural to plants or microbes.

We tend to think of the supernatural as a line drawn between fact and fantasy, but it lies between what we can and cannot explain or accept as possible. What is natural or supernatural depends only upon where in the scale of insight and knowledge the observer stands.

If mineral may become living matter when touched by a 'higher' realm, is it so absurd to allow that another 'higher' realm may yet exist, able to touch and charge us with supe-natural spiritual life? Many have felt it and know it exists.

But caution! In this realm dark and light are mortally pitted. Both teams beckon. Choose your side with great care! Expediency, comfort and compromise make easy bedfellows that dull or destroy our ability to choose between mere glitter and the supernatural reality of enduring gold. What a choice to miss!

The Next Dimension

Stand at the portals of all space
And gaze upon the Universe.
Observe its gradual spinning grace
And see all matter intersperse
The bounds of all Creation.

Now, stand within the rim of time;
Upon the out-most world,
Then search throughout all space sublime
And you will find no clue unfurled
To hint — the Next Dimension.

Thus may a man observe a flower
With science or with art.
But the plant has not the power
To respond in slightest part
Or sense man's life of thought.

So thought is of another sphere
From every plant concealed,
Yet subtle thought will not make clear
The other realm man needs revealed,
To glimpse the Next Dimension.

Another life, just as concealed
As thought is from the plant,
Exists for all, and stands Revealed!
O happy Man! Be jubilant,
And grasp the Next Dimension!

Stand at the portals of all space
Look back upon the Universe.
Observe its gradual spinning grace
And smile, for you may now converse
Direct with all Creation!

Tirley 06 09 91

Strange Gifts

I recall the calm of days
As the keen eyed, clock-ticking minutes
Peeled away the intervening time.

And gradually the calm is stirred
By the currents of recurrent fears,
And memories and thoughts that trickle
Blood- warm through the chinks in one's armour
To freeze into sharp shards
When they reach within.

And here is the day.
Mere hours strew their few minutes
Before the moment at the core of my concern.

And yet God has worked his calm
On all this.

I dress and go, knowing only that
It is His strange gift of healing
And deeper growth that I go to grasp,
And to unwrap.

And as I do, the calm steadies into peace

Staines 02 04 97

Grave

The dribble of earth through your fingers
Falls hollow against the brass plaque
Screwed to the coffin top,
And raw earth peeps past
The artificial grass mat
Draped into the hole
To disguise the reality of burial.

Nor is the excavated earth
Allowed to speak clearly
Of its cause, or destiny.
It too is covered
Lest death should seem too stark.

Yet we must face this journey.
It is our only certitude,
But we are coy,
Metering out our grief
Against the gradual ritual
Of hymns and prayers.

But then the handful of dirt
Splashes across the coffin
And the dead within don't stir.
This is no noise for them
In total silence.
But is for us our last contact,
The noise we carry away, the end,
If we do not see the light beyond
And note the passing of life
From here to there.

Staines 18 03 9~

Psalm I

My soul declares the glory of the Lord,
From every fibre issues calm.
The voice within has no urgent note,
And trust suffuses all my thoughts.

What shall I say?
Who shall worry me?
Where is there cause for concern?

Power lies in His hands,
The hands that lift me.
Love streams from His heart
And compassion covers all my iniquities.

I have not a claim on these,
Weak and sinful as I am,
But He looks on the motive my weak heart would follow.
And washes out my stain
To clad me again in white.

Now I long for a greater strength
A closer walk.
Come, Lord, Show me more.

CEA. Harefield, Saturday 6th September 1997

Moscow Morning

Moscow spring morning sun
Presses through the froth of foliage
Above the pedestrian packed,
Hard pressed grass less park below,
Strewn with slender trees
That reach for the sky
Between these encircling Soviet walls.

Impassive, the brick bland and high
Blocks of flats stare,
While secret life expands within
To the limit of grudging opportunity
Behind the scruffy halls and stairs.

The green glow filters into apartments
Uninvited, and below,
I n the earth packed grassless park
Early morning dogs sniff meaningfully
At yesterday's trees, and each other,
For day to day data on who's who.
Their early owners pull
And patient pets give way reluctantly
As a free dog barks his jeering provocation.

And above it all, high in the background air,
The rush hour rises as an offering.
Gradually this green enclosed
Sun can-opened world yields
To the penetration of pets and people;
And the Moscow day drops into gear.

35,000ft , Riga-London, 21 05 96

A Simple Man's Carol

I sing His song; just a simple man,
Who know not where it leads,
But He on high
Knows where and why
And answers all of my needs.

I sing His song; just a simple man,
Seeking to know His will;
With tearful sigh, Or joyous cry,
It clarifies, when I'm still.

I sing His song; just a simple man,
Who listens hard to hear
To catch the clue . ...
Find what to do.
Eager to know: How to steer?

So sing His song, as simple men,
Carolling live-life long!
His catchy tune,
Is our great boon,
For showing us right from wrong.

So sing His song, all simple men,
Accept God's way to re-build.
This tortured World,
Needs Love unfurled!
The challenge of life! Fulfilled!

So sing His song; all simple men,
In faith and fellowship, act!
Join in the fray,
Help win, God's way!
Make Heaven on Earth a fact!

CEA950125. TWI8 2AJ

Cold Turkey

The Bosphorus
Was for us
A Pull —
To Istanbul.
But Marmara
On camera
Was forlorn —
Like the Golden Horn.
And Istanbul
Was chocker full!
I just grew anti 'em
In Byzantium!

'It's Grotto! Man!'
This ancient Ottoman.
A Constant of people —
Called Constantinople!
It must be a consequence
Of being in Continent(s).

28 02 94 Staines

Druggist

Best be chary,
Very wary
Of a mad apothecary
Who proposes
Daily doses
Leading to apotheosis!

Sheep Walking

By dale and pasture, hill and rut
I roved in rural rapture but,
'T was not a sheep perched on the crag;
Just a bloated placcy bag.

Next, a flock, in landscape bonny,
Was in fact mere *roche moutonnée*!
My country scene of resting flocks
Turned out to be - just resting rocks!

Seemingly, the rural idyll,
It's a stage set! One big fiddle!
Agricultural trompe d'oeil

Insomniacs! Abandon sleep!
If you rely on counting sheep!

The Letter

'Twas late upon a heavy een
that from its folded form
the cloudy scream broke from its seal
to terrorise the dawn.

And so to sleep: unslept for fear
the parents stove to quell...
Had the dark their daughter snatched...
or stood she sane and well?

Unfolded now the folded sheet; a
scream as still as stealth
silent till the eye flick't oer
  to slow exhume its wealth.

Ah here! The aching arching heart,
and there, youth's straining ear
intent upon life's quandary quest,
  to catch what it might hear.

So slowly, came our quaking calm
for from this ferment spew,
within the foaming spate of words,
  ideals first bathed, then grew.

No scream, no folded form of fear,
just youth on honest quest,
ranging for the truth from life,
to found it - on the best.

(c) CEA/930206/TW18 2AJ

Accident in the Park

The swing is swung.
>   The dust is riz...

I wonder where the kiddie is?

Ah there! Beneath the seat the nonce,
With growing bump - upon his bonce!

Moral -

The swing when swung
>   kinetic is!

And gravity a funny biz...

So thoughtfully your kid ensconce...
Lest bumps assail him - more than once!

Grenville

The white hot moon lay glimmering
On the black silk skin of the pond
While on the far shore, mid fern galore,
Stood an upturned root that served as a door
To the burrow that lay beyond.

Deep in the damp of the burrow
A frog stood rehearsing his grin,
While on the far shore, in hat of straw,
His lover dreamed of his knock on the door,
And her blush, as she lets him in.

"Walk there? No! Too pedestrian!
But hopping would risk ridicule.
Should I ride a bike, or brave the pike,
And arrive, dripping brawn, all Tarzan like?
Now THAT's how to come across 'cool'!"

"Oh! There!" said his love, "I see him!
He's swimming! How fine his physique!"
Her voice, light and fair, on mid-nighty air,
Flew to the swimmer who, full with despair,
Shouted "PIKE! My outlook is bleak!"

"Grenville! Oh, Grenville! Swim harder!
My tasty sweet frog! Oh! My charm'd!
Head for the bank ... !" But with that HE SANK!
The moon closed over;- then dripping and dank
He strode ashore grinning, unharmed!

'You cheater! You toad! You scoundrel!'
I'll never believe what you say!
You said you were dead, but here instead,
Your grin goes around both sides of your head;
While I was just fainting away!

'My love! My little potato!
Oh, my sweet, come into my arms!
They are wet I know, but time will show
That though I've wet arms, I've fine legs you know,
So take me without any qualms!'
She did, and they live refinely,
In the hole on the bank beyond.
(Behind an old root, where ferns still shoot.)
And they dance the while, to the foxglove flute;
With tadpoles galore, in the pond!

Staines 04 11 92

Giles, the Potential Pirate

Giles was very determined.
Giles was quite dead set.
Piracy really appealed to him,
A Pirate he'd be yet,

Giles enrolled in Pirate School.
Giles was not afraid!
He learned how to balance a parrot:
Achieved the highest grade!

Giles worked hard at plundering.
Giles learned all he should,
And soon swashed a buckle much better
Than all the others could!

Giles was 'Curdle Cup' winner;
Giles just scooped the prize.
His "Yo! Ho! HO!" could curdle the blood,
In those of half his size.

Giles looked BAD in an eye patch;
Giles could really LEER,
While watching a ship mate walk the plank ... !
Smirking from ear to ear!

Giles got 'Piracy'. (Honours)
Giles, P.I.R.A.T.E., was cruel!
But the only work poor Giles could get
Was Life Guard, at a pool!

Giles was most disappointed.
Giles was quite cast down.
(It's awfully awkward to plunder,
Being well known round town!)

Giles was VERY unhappy.
Giles became ... withdrawn.
No Jolly Roger. No treasure, just ...
Poolside! Peeled, like a prawn!

Giles is watching the adverts.
Giles will soon be gone ...
To greener piratical pastures,
To BE a Pirate on!

Giles still says he's determined,
Giles is still dead set!
Piracy really appeals to him,
A Pirate - he WILL be yet!

Staines 16 11 92

Revenge!

I threw my haggis in the sky:
It fell to earth, I know not why.

I wanted it to fly and fly,
So heft it up, twice as high!

My haggis didn't seem to try.
Just plummeted! Vertic'ly!

So gradually, by and by
I KNEW my haggis wouldn't fly!

I took it home. I didn't cry,
But cooked and ate it, in a pie.

TO TEACH IT A LESSON!

Staines 31 10 9~

Sir Knight

I tell the tale of an aged knight
No longer at his peak,
But one so bold that in days of old
He could make the strongest meek.

He won his spurs in courageous wars
Waged upon sullen men,
And he bore his helm throughout the realm
With a pride undaunted then.

His deeds stand out in the lists of time,
Clear 'gainst the yellowed page,
For he ran his race at Tilting pace
That slowed not a lot with age.

But time takes it's toll; we all succumb;
Teeth grow loose in the jaw;
His strength today is not ebbed away,
Just housed in his heart far more.

Now from afar come the strongest knights
To talk with one so greyed.
Not one removed, but one fully proved
By the cards and dice life played.

I would you could meet with old Sir Knight
Who's spurs are deep ideas.
Now he wields his heart with mighty art
That's the wonder of his peers.

I tell the tale of this aged knight,
Not a sad tale, let it be said.
His lingering touch will count for much
Long after this knight lies dead.

Staines 02 10 92

Trickledown

On cowslip downs do diamond dews
Collect against the sun,
On morning blades of meadow green;
Pure trickledown and run.

And from the battled blades of green
The larking windlet strips
Night's regal jewels, one by one
To moist earth's luscious lips.

'And so it is that God provides.
His purposes? Who sees?
But this I know; by dewdrops grow
All things that do us please.

On cowslip downs do diamond dews
Collect against the sun
On His command it all transpires
Pure, trickledown - and run.

Tirley Garth 27 09 9~

Following the Team

Do you stand behind the barriers,
Do you raise your gusty shout
And cheer the team you're rooting for
Until your throat gives out?

Do you follow all their matches?
Do you know their next venue?
And will you follow faithfully
Until unable to?

Do you sell your team to others?
Do you work to make new fans?
And thrive on what you're doing
Until you fill the stands?

Do you long to see them Victors?
Do you yearn to see them great?
And do you see they won't be
Until you don't spectate?

Do you only want spectators?
Do you win - by cheering on,
And yelling for your players
Until their chance is gone?

Do you mind about them winning?
Do you want to mould the way,
And influence the outcome ... ?
You won't, until you play!

So join the game and sweat it,
Put in your best throughout,
For then, you change the outcome,
 And wrest victory from rout.

When God, as your team captain,
Asks you by name, to play,
Will you choose to stay spectating,
Or kit-up, and join the fray?

Staines 15 08 92

Conversation

The water chats between old rocks
A lively conversation
And tells of fells far off up-stream.
Then, striped by tree shadows,
It pulls cool though pools
To laugh silver in the shallow places.

And trees the while lean over,
As if intent upon the tale,
Nodding in gentle agreement,
Like Ancients by the fire.

We are irrelevant we,
With our boots and knapsacks and ideas.
We are just a point of light
Registered on the dark canopy of time.

This conversation is not for us.
 It is the Universe talking back
Its constant praise to God.

Dedicated to Judith Curtis, on her Birthday
CEA. Grand Canyon, Crimea 160499

Listening

Lord!

I'm deaf. So deaf. Call loudly Lord!
Give me the courage of your word.

When I can hear Lord, I will do
Whatever daily comes from you!

Hark!

A still small voice insistently
Sets forth the truth in front of me.
Another voice asserts, quite clear,
Everything I'd rather hear.
If I grow deaf to truth, and reel
Through Sin that numbs,
I cease to feel, (except the things I deem my right)
Insensitive to others plight.
Yet 'others first' feels too austere
'Obedience' does not endear.
It sounds as if I must forego
The egocentric way I know:
To live a different kind of role,
And change 'self' for another goal.

Lord!

I'm deaf. So deaf.
Call loudly Lord!
Give me the courage of your word.
Direct my head and heart to range,
To seek your will, to make the change
Away from selfish natured me
Towards a close kinship with thee!

Come!

I know your needs, the pain, the tears,
The yawning chasm filled with fears,
The aches that cling to hearts desire,
The sense of want that sears like fire.
Come fearful faithless; walk with me.
Step out in Faith, leave me to see.
My call is quiet; not hard to hear
When hearts listen, its ever there.
Pray; be quiet.
Of heart be still.
Seek my guidance;
then do my will.

CEA 78

Erik Andren (1938-2008)

Architect, inventor, pilot and poet, Erik Andren was a polymath, an original thinker whose inquisitive mind was interested in everything from physics to psychology. Born in Batu Gaja, Malaysia in 1938, his childhood was thrown into confusion by a congenital heart condition—and World War II.

Andren's father was an aero-engineer in Malaysia, but as the Japanese advanced down the Malay Peninsula, the three-year-old Erik was put into boarding school in Britain. After the war, his mother took him to Kodaikanal hill resort in south India, to a climate favourable to his health. They travelled to John Hopkins University Hospital in Baltimore, in search of treatment for his heart, from where he was referred to Guy's Hospital in London. There, in 1950, aged 12, he was the twelfth ever open heart surgery patient in the UK, lying in those days on a bed of ice.

As a result of these circumstances, Andren attended 14 schools on three continents, showing great intelligence despite coping with dyslexia. He studied architecture at Kingston School of Art, Surrey. He joined a firm of engineers, as architect in residence, designing airline facilities, including catering kitchens and shops, at Heathrow; in Benghazi, Libya; Rome, Italy, and in Geneva, Switzerland; as well as housing in Britain.

In the early 1970s he co-founded an architectural practice with four other partners in Weybridge, Surrey. But they struggled through the first oil shock of 1972, when demand for architects' services slumped, and his partners had to leave. Andren's lateral thinking led to his inventions, including the plastic paper feeder, called Margin Maker, for the first Amstrad computer printers, as well as concepts for an affordable river-based hydro-electric system for developing countries.

Andren's interest in people led him to design and write a Changing Course for aspiring politicians and young professionals in Eastern Europe, in response to the collapse of Soviet communism. Launched in 1993, the Changing Course provides the basis for the Foundations for Freedom (F4F) training programme of the Initiatives of Change movement, based in Caux, Switzerland. It highlights the concepts that underpin the moral and ethical foundations for democratic societies, from first principles to issues of personal integrity and ethical and moral behaviour. It also aims to draw on the sources of inner introspection that lead to inspired action.

Despite his own strong Christian beliefs, Andren was fully aware that others may have no religious affiliations and so focused on the need for each participant to spend time in personal R&D—research and development, reflection and decision-making, and from this draw their own strength and conclusions.

Operating initially from London and more recently from Kiev, Ukraine, Foundations for Freedom, with Andren's thinking at its heart, has delivered 70 courses, each typically lasting a week, to over 1,500 young leaders in 15 central and Eastern European countries as well as in South Africa, India, Canada and Australia. Andren delivered the majority of the initial courses, and ensured that others with similar passion were trained to continue delivery as his health and other commitments made foreign travel more difficult.

One young participant, a music teacher from Romania, was to write: "I didn't know any more what was right and what was wrong and what I was supposed to do. My main values had become money and survival. I found myself unhappy, stressed and very bitter... Now I feel the only thing I really want to do is to give to others the chance that I was given to experience a deep change in life and a new purpose."

An unexpected outcome of the F4F courses was the use of Erik's training manual in a similar "Moral Foundations for Democracy" programme in Sierra Leone, aimed at reintegrating former combatants following the country's civil war.

Andren was a warm-hearted extrovert, a man of passionate conviction, and a poet who wrote on a broad range of subjects, from his children to philosophy. One of his poems, Not the Bitter Men, about Northern Ireland, was read in parliament.

He was a devoted father and surreptitious romantic. He married Sheila Davidson, a medical practitioner from Glasgow, in 1969, after proposing to her on their first meeting after years apart. They were an ideal match sharing their lives and home with many people for almost 40 years. He described Sheila as the string to his kite. They raised their children, Lindy and Ross, in Staines, Middlesex, and moved to Fowlmere, South Cambridgeshire, when Sheila retired. Here he was able to re-ignite his lifelong passion for flying by joining the local gliding club, as well as using his architectural skills to redesign their new home.

At the time of his death, Andren and his daughter, Lindy, were editing a book based on his experiences with the Changing Course, which she will continue to edit for posthumous publication, along with his poetry.

Andren died peacefully in Papworth Hospital, aged 70, from heart failure, after a life lived to the full. He is survived by his wife, two children and his mother. He is remembered fondly by all for his quick laugh, the twinkle in his eyes, and his passion for sharing life's deeper concepts with any that would join his conversation.

Michael Smith

Lightning Source UK Ltd.
Milton Keynes UK
UKHW022242051021
391692UK00006B/241